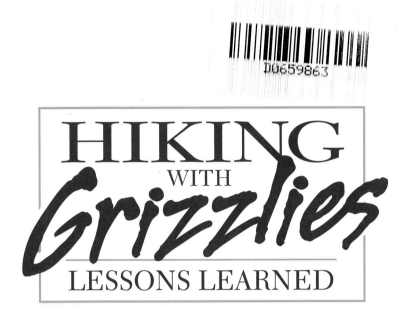

HIKING WITH Grizzlies

LESSONS LEARNED

TIM RUBBERT

Photos by Tim Rubbert

RIVERBEND
PUBLISHING

All bear photos in this book were taken using telephoto lenses
from 200mm to 670mm.

ISBN 13: 978-1-931832-69-4
ISBN 10: 1-931832-69-2
Cover photos by Tim Rubbert
Cover design by Sarah E. Grant, www.sarahegrant.com

RIVERBEND PUBLISHING
P.O. Box 5833
Helena, MT 59604
1-866-787-2363
www.riverbendpublishing.com

DEDICATION

To my brother, Paul Christopher Rubbert,
who was here for too short of a time.
We thank God every day for the gift he gave us.

A grizzly bear is about to cross a hiking trail in Glacier National Park, Montana. Knowing what to do in this situation is one of many lessons in this book.

Acknowledgments

Thank you to the following people, without whose help this book would not have been possible.

My beautiful and creative wife, Suzi: thank you for your love, tolerance and belief in me throughout our years together, and while I've been off on my many expeditions.

My mother and father, Shirley and Len Rubbert: thank you for your nurturing that instilled in me the love of everything wild. To my sister and her husband, Debbie and Brad Nelson, and my brother, Terry Rubbert: thank you for your encouragement.

Jim Cole: thank you for the insight, ideas, and planting the seed for this book. We've got some great memories for our rocking-chair days.

Ben Long: thank you for your endeavors and continuing help. You helped pull it all together.

Mike Fairchild: his work was cut short, but his understanding and inspiration remain.

Thank you to the following people and organizations for their help and support: Chuck Bartlebaugh of Center for Wildlife Information; Big Mountain Resort; John Waller, Ph.D., wildlife biologist, Glacier National Park; and Chris Bernat, Dan Savage, Joseph Brady and Steve Merlino. Last but not least, thanks to Chris Cauble for his perseverance.

A mother grizzly bear and her cubs in Yellowstone National Park.

CONTENTS

Toleration is a trait found in many bears. This female grizzly is calmly watching a crowd of tourists that is watching her and her cubs near a road in Yellowstone National Park.

INTRODUCTION

Encounters with bears, especially grizzlies, have always stirred the imagination. The stories, if usually somewhat exaggerated, have made for some great campfire and barroom tales.

For modern America, the grizzly became a monster on the night of August 13, 1967, when two young women in Glacier National Park, Montana, were killed by two different grizzlies in separate incidents at almost the same time. The "Jaws" effect soon took over most discussions and attitudes about the "Great Bear." A new fear of grizzlies began to spread, even though the vast majority of people had never even seen a grizzly.

Since that August night, most books on bear encounters or attacks, no matter how well intentioned, have not eradicated what I feel is an irrational fear of bears in general and of grizzlies in particular. Rather, the "myth" of the grizzly has not only continued but flourished. Many writers tended to sensationalize grizzly encounters, especially attacks and maulings.

One of the main objectives for writing this book is to dispel the "myth" of the grizzly. I have learned that the grizzly is not a monster. Grizzlies are not out there lurking in the brush, waiting for some hapless souls to wander by so they can jump out and devour them. Conversely, they are not cuddly creatures either. No matter what you've seen on television or read in books and magazines, wild bears are wild bears. To consider them cuddly creatures or attribute human qualities to them exhibits a lack of respect and understanding.

The grizzly normally wants nothing to do with humans and will go out of its way to avoid them. Maulings usually occur through "surprise" encounters; the great bear does not like surprises. People are attacked because the bear feels threatened and reacts defensively. Many bear-related fatalities, including those on August 13, 1967, were the result of habituated and food-conditioned bears.

In simple terms, habituated bears are bears that have become accustomed to the presence of humans. In and of itself, habituation is not necessarily bad. But bears that associate people with food, usually through garbage or by actually getting fed by people, are food-conditioned bears, and food-conditioned bears can be very dangerous. Unfortunately, many food-conditioned bears start out as habituated bears.

Another objective of this book is to lay a foundation for procedures to be utilized to avoid bear encounters and to safely survive an encounter should one occur. I will do this by thoroughly discussing, and in most cases photographically documenting, a number of my encounters with grizzlies. I have learned many lessons through these encounters. I hope my lessons will help influence future human/bear interactions in a positive manner.

Most books on hiking in bear country have been written by authors who have collected information from other people who were involved in bear encounters. Therefore the reader is receiving second- or third-hand information. In this book, the reader receives the information directly from the "horse's mouth." I have had firsthand experiences with bear attacks, bluff charges, and other bear encounters, and I will share those experiences in this book. The advantage is that I can personally describe the bear's behavior in the encounter, including body language, sound, prior activity, etc. I will also explain my behavior and activity directly before, during, and after the encounter.

I make certain conclusions throughout the book. However, I provide enough information for readers to draw their own conclusions or develop their own hypothesis about successful bear avoidance or encounter strategies.

Procedures for avoiding or safely encountering bears are based on a few major elements:
1) Recognition of bear habitat.
2) Recognition of bear sign.
3) Hiking or activity strategy.
4) An encountered bear's behavior.
5) Personal response strategy (also called encounter strategy)
6) Bear spray

Although I will go into greater depth on every element as it relates to each encounter in this book, I will briefly discuss the elements here:

Recognition of bear habitat: being able to recognize bear habitat is an important factor when hiking and camping in bear country. The most significant part of habitat is food. I believe food is the primary motivation for bears, so being able to properly identify bear food will enable you to devise, alter, and execute safe hiking strategies.

Recognition of bear sign: bears leave clues or "signs" of their presence in an area. Signs can include tracks, scat (excrement), diggings, rubbing trees, etc. Proper identification of these signs is crucial to adapting your behavior in bear country and to developing a strategy that takes into account changing and unforeseen conditions.

Hiking or activity strategy (what you do to avoid encountering a bear): for any activity in bear country, one should have a preplanned strategy to avoid close encounters. The primary focus should be to avoid surprising a bear, especially a grizzly. The best way to avoid surprising a bear is to make noise. Noise makes any potential bear in the vicinity aware of your presence. Notice I say "potential." If you see a bear that is unaware of your presence, making noise may not be the best strategy. What kind of noise, how much, when, and how long will be discussed in detail.

The most important part of any strategy is to be prepared for any possibility. In other words, take nothing for granted; be alert at all times. Being alert basically means being in tune with your surroundings. This is easier said than done considering the human mind's ability to "wander." I try to concentrate on using most of my senses when hiking in grizzly country. Most people use their sight to pick out possible danger. This is no different for me. However, I continually scan from side to side and ahead on the trail and directly towards my feet, looking for both bears and bear sign. There have been many times when I walked right by a bear without seeing it because my focus was towards the easiest place to look (toward the trail in front of me) instead of the most logical (the close areas on either side of me).

Most people (including myself at times) expect that if they encounter a grizzly, it will be right on the trail in front of them. Actually most encounters occur with a bear near the trail but not on it, and many times the bear is hidden by brush or other cover. That is why many times I will stop, be still, and scan and listen in all directions. Not only have I seen bears that I just passed, but I have heard bears that I could not see. Bears are not necessarily silent animals, especially moving through brush. I also try to be aware of the wind direction. Obviously wind on my back helps carry my smell to any bears ahead of me, alerting them to my approach. Wind in my face means I must make more noise and take extra precautions.

An encountered bear's behavior: the most important thing to do when you encounter a bear is to stay still (freeze) and remain calm (easier said than done) and watch the bear's reaction to you. How the bear behaves will dictate what you should do. Remaining calm, as will be seen, is the biggest factor to safely ending an encounter. Never run! The last three people killed by grizzlies in Glacier National Park were probably involved in some evasive maneuvering that included running.

Personal response strategy (what you do when you encounter a bear): a bear's reaction to your presence can vary from seeming indifference to extreme agitation, to immediate charge, to immediate escape, or anything in between. This means you must be ready to react appropriately to a number of different scenarios, some of which could be life threatening. If a charge is not occurring or does not seem imminent, removing yourself from the situation is the number-one priority. It should be noted that most bear encounters end rather quickly with the bear running away or moving out of the area. It is when the bear remains, rather than flees, that your decisions are of the utmost importance.

Bears, especially grizzlies, usually attack because they feel threatened, and bears will usually let you know when they feel threatened. These warning "signs" will be discussed in more detail throughout the book. Your goal is to diminish or eliminate your "threat" to the bear.

Bear spray: I am a firm believer in bear spray. I had to use it in two extreme situations which are described in this book. Carrying bear spray does not guarantee your safety nor should it be considered "brains in a can." The main advantage of carrying bear spray is that it gives you another option, and you are more apt to remain calm because you know you have this option. Of course, bear spray is most effective when you know how to use it properly, and I provide specific advice for carrying and using bear spray.

Using numerous examples, I will describe how I used the above guidelines to avoid or survive different types of bear encounters. The vast majority of my bear encounters in this book were within 50 yards of the bear, which most authorities and I consider a critical range. However, some discussion will be made of encounters at greater distances (50 to 100 yards).

Most of the encounters in this book are documented with photographs which, I hope, will give the reader insight on what to expect in an actual encounter. Of course, I do not go hiking with the purpose of directly encountering a bear. My main objective is to learn as much as possible about grizzlies and their habitats in the least intrusive manner. My main strategy is to find safe places to view relatively open areas where I can observe grizzlies from safe and unobtrusive distances. It is when I have been hiking to and from such areas that most of my bear encounters have occurred. I only take photos when I feel it is safe for both me and the bear. In many cases I have not taken photos either because it was the last thing on my mind or because I did not want to cause the bear to change its behavior.

Some people have and will continue to criticize me for intruding into the bear's domain. Other activities are probably more intrusive, especially when conducted by people who have little or no awareness of bears or their habitats. I believe my observations and experiences will, in the long run, help people understand their own roles and impacts when traveling in bear country.

I have been observing and photographing grizzlies for more than 20 years. In that time I have hiked thousands of miles (over 10,000 miles in the last eight years alone) and experienced more than 1,500 grizzly sightings (not all different bears) in the Lower 48 states. I have done volunteer work on grizzlies for the United States Biological Survey in Denali National Park, Alaska.

Most of my observations have taken place in the Northern Continental Divide Ecosystem in Montana, which includes Glacier National Park, the Whitefish Range, and the Bob Marshall Wilderness Complex. To a lesser extent I have made observations in the Greater Yellowstone Ecosystem, including Yellowstone National Park. I am in the backcountry as much as possible.

The grizzly is majestic, beautiful, intelligent, and powerful, while at the same time gentle and shy. Viewing a grizzly is the epitome of a wilderness experience. Every time I see a grizzly, it is like I am seeing one for the first time. Backcountry bears are especially a treat to see, since witnessing them occurs in an environment untouched by man. I never tire of the experience. It is a passion that keeps growing stronger within me.

Bears often use hiking trails. This young grizzly is checking out serviceberry bushes along the trail. Note the long front claws that are typical of grizzly bears.

CHAPTER 1
FIRST ENCOUNTERS

All bear encounters are memorable, but first encounters are especially memorable for a number of reasons. First, they often provide a person with a new experience that is usually far different from any preconceived notions. Second, a person can learn a lot about themselves and how they react in potentially dangerous situations. Third and most important, in my case anyway, you can do some real boneheaded things and still survive.

I classify the three encounters in this chapter as first encounters because of the newness of the situations to me and because of the important knowledge I gained and the mistakes I made. Ignorance is not bliss when it comes to hiking in bear country. Even though I had hiked extensively in bear country and had seen many bears prior to these encounters, I had not experienced a surprise meeting with either a black bear or a grizzly. Reading bear books made me aware of the risks but did not necessarily make me appreciate the full extent of all possible scenarios. I hope this book does a better job at preparing readers for bear encounters.

AUGUST 1989
Apgar Lookout Trail, Glacier National Park

My wife, Suzi, and I had been camping in Glacier for five days. We had done much driving and hiking in the park, looking for bears without much success. It was a clear sunny day, so we decided to hike the Apgar Lookout Trail. Our intention was not to look for bears. Instead, we wanted to hike the trail because we had never hiked it before and had heard the view from the top was outstanding.

The trail was about three miles long and climbed about 1,800 feet in elevation. Once the trail started to climb, it consisted of three long inclines divided by two switchbacks. We started the hike in the early afternoon, taking our time. We observed no bear sign on the way up. Except for a few huckleberry bushes with berries, there was nothing to indicate that bears might be in the area. When we reached the top, the views in every direction were breathtaking. We spent some time there, taking in the vista and relaxing in the sun. Then we started a leisurely hike down to our truck.

Suzi was in the lead. We rounded the top switchback and began the middle descent. Halfway down, Suzi suddenly stopped, pointed, and said there was movement just ahead to the left of the trail. I immediately saw two small, black shapes rocket up two separate trees. We knew what was happening. We started looking for the black bear mother in the dark underbrush, and then we heard a noise that neither of us had ever heard before. The best way to describe the noise, and the first thing I thought of when I heard it, is the sound of a handsaw cutting a dry, 2 x 4 stud. It even had the same rhythm.

Now I could see the mother bear at the base of the two trees her cubs had shot up. My first thought was that she might be sick because of the seemingly strange sounds she was making. However, I soon realized she was making warning sounds. I would hear these sounds many times in the following years.

I now describe these warning sounds as "huffing," and both grizzlies and black bears make the sound. Some bear writers describe the sounds as "woofing,""but the sounds are not like the "woof" of a dog. They are somewhat like the alarm snort of a white-tailed deer, although not as nasal. It is a distinct, blowing noise.

As I continued to watch the mother bear, Suzi backed up the trail and disappeared around a bend. I took a few photos of the bear as it continued huffing. Then I backed up the trail to see where Suzi had gone. She had climbed a tree and was hoping for my return. Climbing a tree would not stop a black bear, but it made Suzi feel safe. I realized she had more sense and had recognized the danger. I, on the other hand, had been more interested in the bear's behavior than forming a correct response strategy. Black bears with cubs have mauled people and should not be taken lightly. I definitely made a mistake and only had the bear's patience to thank for a positive outcome. Her cubs were safely up trees, and I did not approach her. Had I pushed her due to my ignorance, events may have been different.

It was about six o'clock and we didn't want to spend any more time where we were. After waiting about 10 minutes, I took out my bear spray and walked back down the trail to check on the bears. They were still there. The mother started huffing again, and the cubs were still in the trees. I went back to Suzi and we decided to bushwhack down the mountainside to the lower section of the trail. We did this without much difficulty and finished our hike.

I basically look back at this encounter as a major learning experience. Little did I know that every encounter is a major learning experience.

NOVEMBER 1989
Going to the Sun Road, Glacier National Park

It was a mild fall and the Going to the Sun Road was still open. My wife and I drove to a spot where a week earlier we had seen grizzlies digging. As we approached the area, I pulled over and scanned the open mountainside. Two grizzly siblings were digging in an open area. We drove up the road and stopped at a pullout.

B211

We were now about 300 yards below the bears. We got out of the truck and as I walked to the back of the truck to get my spotting scope and tripod, I heard a loud "huff." I now knew what that sound meant. I looked directly across the road to the sound, expecting to see a black bear. To my amazement, the sound came from a female grizzly with two cubs-of-the-year, only 30 feet away. I turned to Suzi and said, as calmly as I could, "Get back in the truck."

I was astonished. That bear could have been on top of me in an instant before I ever knew what was happening. I began to decipher a revelation into the true nature of bears, and of grizzlies in particular. I never saw or had any indication there might be a bear that close when we got out of the truck. Looking at photo B211 you can understand why. I took this photo after we got back in the truck, and I use this photo as an example of how people can be surprisingly close to a bear without being aware of its presence. People frequently hike by bears without ever knowing it. Many times the bear, when it knows you are approaching, will hide until you are gone. Then it will continue doing what it was doing before you approached. This is why it is so important to make noise when hiking. I also look behind me every so often. Occasionally I have seen bears that I have just walked by.

The grizzly bears seemed fairly habituated, and they continued digging while people drove by or stopped. The cubs stayed near their mother and seemed unconcerned with anyone's presence. No one else got out of their vehicle, and it seemed this behavior was the key to the bears' comfort zone near the road.

The event taught me that an encounter can occur in the unlikeliest places and also when least expected. When hiking or recreating in bear country, the fewer preconceived ideas and expectations you have, the more appropriate your responses will be. In other words, when you are expecting anything, you will be less surprised and startled. Panic will be less likely and more level-headed thinking will occur.

JULY, 1990
West Side, Glacier National Park

I took a four-mile hike (one-way) on the west side of Glacier to check on a huckleberry crop. I started the hike at 3 pm on a clear, hot day which was fairly typical for late July. About a mile and a half up the trail I encountered some rather productive huckleberry bushes with large, ripe berries. I couldn't resist; I began to gorge myself. As my hands turned dark purple from the berries, a couple of hikers approached and also began to pick berries. After talking with them for a while, I continued my hike. The lower half of the trail where I had been picking berries was in a rather thick forest. I spotted some berry-filled bear scat on the trail, but it appeared old. About halfway up the trail, the forest was cut with avalanche chutes. After about nine such chutes the trail broke into the open.

I sat down and cooled off. I surveyed the surrounding huckleberry bushes and saw that the berries were not yet ripe at that elevation. I viewed the surrounding open areas and mountainsides without seeing any bears and decided it was time to head back. I was thinking about the area where I had picked berries. I figured I had time to pick more berries on the way down. As I neared the ripe berries in the forest, I noticed that the scat I had seen on the way up had either been pushed or scraped off the trail. The only explanation I could think of was that the hikers had kicked it off the trail. I continued hiking and soon rounded one of the many blind bends in the trail.

Right away I heard a loud "HUFF!" I looked up, expecting to see a black bear in the huckleberry bushes. To my complete astonishment, the sound came from a rather large grizzly. It was about 40 feet in front of me and just to the left of the trail. I was dumbfounded. I had heard and read that grizzlies were rarely seen in thick forests. Boy, did I have a lot to learn! I grabbed the bear spray that was in my back pocket, pulled off the safety lever, and backed up the trail away from the grizzly.

The grizzly took off through the thick cover, not directly away from me but at an angle above me. I lost sight of it but I could hear it crashing through the brush. I started climbing a nearby tree, thinking the bear could return and I wouldn't have much room on the trail to maneuver. I also would feel safer in the tree. As I was climbing, a branch rubbed across my face, flinging my glasses into space. Now I couldn't see a damn thing. As I moved higher in the tree, I heard a loud "huff" which scared the hell out of me and almost made me fall. Then I realized I had accidentally hit the trigger on the bear spray. I had been carrying the bear spray in one hand as I climbed the tree. Bear spray, when it goes off, sounds very much like the "huff" of a bear. I was lucky I didn't spray myself in the face.

So there I was, about 20 feet high in a lodgepole pine, unable to see, wondering what to do next. Then dark clouds, thunder, and lightening approached. I said to myself, "Oh this is great." I couldn't spend much more time in the tree. It was about 7 pm. There was plenty of daylight left, but the approaching storm and the need to locate my glasses dictated that I get the hell out of there.

I didn't know if the bear was still in the vicinity, and I couldn't see it if it was. When I didn't hear any brush moving, I started yelling in hopes that if the bear was still around, the noise would encourage it to leave. After a few minutes of yelling, I climbed down the tree. I cautiously began searching for my glasses while staying alert to any noise or movement. Thankfully, I found my glasses rather quickly. I made a quick attempt to find the bear spray safety lever, but I didn't see it. I wanted to get out of there as quickly as possible.

I started hiking at a brisk pace, yelling the whole time. I didn't want to run into that same bear or any other bear for that matter. It started to rain but luckily a big storm didn't materialize. I made it back to my vehicle in about half an hour.

I obviously made numerous mistakes on this hike. I acted like a typical tourist without a clue. Thanks to this bear's tolerance, nothing serious happened although I probably scared the heck out of the poor creature due to my lack of awareness and repeated yelling. Looking back on the encounter, valuable lessons can be learned.

First, an important clue was provided at the very beginning when I ran into the ripe huckleberries. If I could easily gorge on the berries, so could a bear. The scat in the trail was also an important sign. It told me a bear had been in the area. The scat appeared old, but combined with the presence of ripe berries, I should have realized that bears could certainly still be there.

Second, as I approached the berry area on the way down, I was not taking the proper precautions. I should have been making more noise and been more alert, especially when approaching blind curves in the trail.

Third, I assumed only black bears were in thickly wooded areas. This was a totally faulty assumption, since grizzlies can be found anywhere, especially if food is available. Grizzlies are usually not seen in wooded areas simply because they are harder to see, not because they are absent. And when grizzlies are seen in wooded areas, it is usually at close range.

This bear encounter changed my thinking immensely. Ever since, I have tried to avoid having specific expectations and preconceived assumptions. The more I learn about bears the more I realize how much I don't know about bears. My hiking and personal response strategies are constantly changing as I gain new knowledge, especially from personal experiences.

Thinking about all of these "first encounters" has led me to believe I was a somewhat slow learner. Some people may not have the luxury of the bears' tolerance and patience. For some people a first encounter could be their last. It is the purpose of this book to provide the reader with information, through my own experiences, to help you avoid these potentially dangerous situations.

A yearling grizzly bear stands on its hind legs. The stance is usually to better see, smell or hear, not an aggressive posture.

CHAPTER 2
BEAR BASICS

In order for the reader to gain a better understanding of bear encounters, it is imperative to explain two components of grizzly bear ecology: habitat and bear sign. I believe the single most important factor of grizzly habitat is food. Other factors include water and cover. Bear sign is the evidence bears leave of their presence. Knowledge of bear habitat and bear sign is extremely important in determining the likelihood of an encounter.

Food

Grizzlies eat an incredibly wide variety of foods. Most people believe that grizzlies eat nothing but meat, but in many ecosystems, especially Glacier and Denali national parks, grizzlies eat mostly plants. Meat in any form is usually only available on a seasonal or opportunistic basis. For that reason I will mostly cover plant food. Food from animal sources will be covered more extensively in Chapter 12. Plants and plant derivatives eaten by grizzlies vary by location and season. Only those plants that my friend Jim Cole and I have actually witnessed bears consuming will be discussed.

Glacier lilies (also known as dogtooth violets) and spring beauties are widespread and abundant in the northern Rocky Mountains of the Lower 48 states. The yellow flowers of the glacier lily and the small white flowers of the spring beauty blossom right after the snow melts in early spring. Depending on the elevation, the blossoming can occur anytime between May and August. When blooming, we have seen grizzlies grazing on the flowers and leaves. After the flowers have diminished for the season with the leaves turning yellow and drying up,

B823

B1091

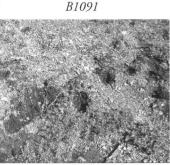

B862

B1093

we have witnessed grizzlies digging the roots and bulbs of each plant. Photo B823 shows the springtime diggings of glacier lily roots next to a trail. Photo B1091 shows fall diggings. Glacier lilies are one of the most widespread and abundant foods in the Northern Continental Divide Ecosystem (NCDE) in northern Montana. Glacier lilies are also present in the Greater Yellowstone Ecosystem (GYE) around Yellowstone National Park, but we have not seen any evidence of utilization by grizzlies there.

Another important plant that blossoms in the spring is the biscuitroot. The flowers are very small. Grizzlies dig up the roots of the blooming plant, but the diggings (Photo B862) are not as extensive as glacier lily diggings. Also notice the rocky soil, a common feature of biscuitroot sites. We have seen evidence of biscuitroot utilization only from mid spring to late spring. Utilization does not seem to be as widespread as glacier lily usage. It is, however, utilized in both the GYE and NCDE.

In the GYE another spring food is pocket gophers. Grizzlies dig for the animal and for the pocket gopher's cache of seeds and other plant parts. Photo B1093 shows a close-up of one of these diggings. Notice the snow. We have noticed that when other food sources, such as biscuitroot, are not available, bears are more apt to dig for pocket gophers and their caches. Pocket gophers are widespread throughout much of the NCDE but we have never personally seen pocket gophers utilized there.

During the summer different kinds of berries ripen. Where available, berries are some of the richest sources of fat-producing carbohydrates for bears. In the NCDE, huckleberries (and related berries of vaccinium) are among the most sought after berries (Photo B1217). In the GYE huckleberries are not nearly as abundant. Other berries appearing in both ecosystems include soapberries (also called buffalo berries), chokecherries, serviceberries, wild raspberries, kinnickinnic (also called bearberries), twinberries, and mountain ash. This is not a complete list of berries but merely the berries we have seen bears eating.

B1217

Grizzlies utilize berries more heavily when berries are abundant and thick in localized areas. If the berries are too widespread or too sparse, requiring too much energy to obtain them, they are not utilized as much. In some years this results in bears wandering farther in search of other food resources. In "bad" berry years, bears may be seen in areas they normally don't frequent. Some people believe such sightings indicate an increasing bear population when in reality the population is stressed and may actually be declining, especially if berry failures happen in successive years.

B945

When berries ripen at lower elevations, hikers must take extra care. This is because the cover or vegetation is usually thicker at lower elevations, making it more difficult to see bears at distances. As summer proceeds, berries begin to ripen at higher elevations where there are fewer trees and less cover. There will be more opportunities to see bears at distances, but caution must still be exercised, especially around pockets of thick cover.

The serviceberry is another popular food, especially in the NCDE. Serviceberries do not seem to be as sought after as huckleberries, but when they are abundant, they may be utilized as much or more. The leaves of the bushes turn yellow or gold as fall approaches.

When bears eat berries, we have noticed two methods. When berries, especially huckleberries, are abundant on individual bushes, a bear use its front paw to place a branch in its mouth and then strips off the berries in one motion. When berries are not thick, bears bite individual berries off the bushes. This technique is seen in photo B945, where a grizzly is eating serviceberries.

B1094

B974

Mountain ash berries are not particularly favored by grizzlies but they will be consumed when little else is available. These berries are consumed much more by black bears. Kinnickinnic berries grow very low to the ground. The special nature of these berries allows them to be available anytime of the year. Photo B1094 shows a grizzly eating kinnickinnic berries in October when no other berries were available. We have also seen bears eating kinnickinnic berries in the spring. Photo B974 shows a grizzly eating chokecherries from a bush in the background that it had just stripped. This photo was taken in September. The bear is standing over a wild rose bush. The bear later ate the rosehips on the bush.

These examples represent just a small portion of what grizzlies eat. The most important factors to remember when you come across possible bear foods are abundance and concentration. When both of those factors are present, there is a greater probability of a bear in the area. When both factors are present with favored food such as huckleberries, many bears can be present. One day Jim Cole and I saw 24 bears within one square mile, all feeding on huckleberries. We conclusively identified twenty-two of the bears as grizzlies and we presumed the other two bears were also grizzlies. Because of the potentially dangerous situation in which we found ourselves, we left before we could identify the two "unknowns." When food resources are plentiful, it is not uncommon to see grizzlies and black bears in close proximity, sharing the resources.

Water

When discussing grizzlies, water plays an important factor in determining their presence. Two basic components are involved. First, since hydration is essential, water sources must be present for a grizzly to survive. When hiking in an area devoid of water, in liquid or solid form, the chances of seeing a bear are much lower unless the bear is just passing through. Additionally, water increases the chances for food to be available and increases the likelihood of a bear spending time in an area. If there are rich food sources, water can exist some distance away and the area will still attract bears. I have seen bears move several thousand vertical feet for water. Some food sources, such as berries, can provide significant amounts of water.

B1097

Second, and sometimes more important, grizzlies love water for playing and cooling off. I have seen more grizzlies near or in water for these purposes than for drinking. Photo B1097 shows a black bear cooling off on a dry, hot day. During hot conditions, the best time to witness bears near large bodies of water is late morning to late afternoon. The same period is optimal for viewing grizzlies in patches of snow and snowfields. For this reason extra caution should be taken near these areas.

Cover

Cover is another important component of bear habitat. Cover can take many forms, but it consists primarily of forested areas and/or thick vegetation where a grizzly can conceal itself. Cover is used by bears for sleeping, cooling, and/or basic security needs. Hiking near cover, especially when prime food sources or water are nearby, calls for extra precautions. Additional noise in areas of cover is always warranted.

M330

The presence of all three components of habitat increases the probability of a bear being present.

Photo M330 provides an example of prime grizzly country. Food (huckleberries) are available in the open areas. Good cover is available for shelter and security, and there is water in the creek bottom.

My hiking strategy emphasizes food resource identification. If there is a suitable food source in the area, the other two components—water and cover—also demand attention.

Bear Sign

Recognition of bear sign is a key element in developing a successful hiking strategy. Bear sign includes scat (excrement), diggings, rubbing trees, tracks, beds, turned over rocks, torn up stumps, and downed trees that have been rolled over or moved.

Scat is probably the bear sign most often encountered. The difference between black bear and grizzly scat is usually one of diameter and volume. Grizzly scat is larger in both categories. However, because of variations in the sizes of bears, even within a species, bear species identification by scat size alone is problematic. Photo B863 shows grizzly biscuitroot scat. Photo B1098 shows presumed grizzly dandelion scat. Notice the can of bear spray for size comparison. Both scats are the same color, but the texture is definitely different.

The main difference between fresh and old bear scat is moisture content. As scat ages, it dries up and falls apart. Take a stick and break apart the scat. If the scat has formed a dry outer crust, it is older. If it doesn't have a crust and appears very moist, it is very recent. If it has rained recently it may be difficult to tell how old the scat is. Recent berry scat usually will be a well-formed pile with berries that appear fresh. Older berry scat looks dry and flattens out, with no fresh-appearing berries.

B863

Diggings are another commonly noticed bear sign. Since the grizzly is one of the best excavators in the animal kingdom, digging is a good indicator of a grizzly rather than a black bear. Some photos of diggings were already presented in the previous section on foods. Photo B847 shows the diggings of a grizzly hunting ground squirrels. These diggings can be encountered from Alaska to Yellowstone. I have seen a grizzly digging a hole so large that it disappeared from sight. Any excavation which causes you to wonder, "Why is the park service tilling a garden in the middle of no-where," is likely the work of a grizzly.

B1098

B847

Bear beds are rarely seen because they are usually located in cover. Photo B672 shows a bear bed. Notice the oval depression in the middle of an excavated area, which is the spot where the bear rests. Also notice the scat sur-rounding the bed but not inside it. This sign speaks volumes. First, this is a grizzly bed, as

B672

B1209

B1213

indicated by the amount of digging and also by the size of the scat. All of the scat is huckleberry scat. The scat at the edge of the bed is a message for visitors. This is a particular bear's bed, and it is used on a regular basis. A bear is probably close by and may be back at any time. This is no place to linger. We did not. We listened to hear if the bear was nearby. Grizzlies eating huckleberries are not particularly quiet. Then we left the way we approached. Any other direction might have led us into the bear whose bed we discovered.

Rubbing trees may be encountered along any trail in grizzly country. Rubbing trees often tell a story. Photo B1209 shows a typical rubbing tree just off a hiking trail. At the base of the tree, on the rubbed side, the ground has been beaten down to the bare earth. This happens when a bear is standing and rubbing its back. The bear's hind feet slide back and forth on the ground as it rubs its back up, down, and sideways. A closer inspection of photo B1213 shows bear hair left on the tree.

Bears rub for a couple of reasons. First, they need to scratch just like any other animal. Second, a common hypothesis is that rubbing trees act as communication posts. Using smells and perhaps marks, bears traveling past the trees can learn if other bears are in the area. In this way rubbing trees may help bears avoid dangerous encounters with other bears. For me, such trees are useful to indicate the amount of bear activity in a particular area and how recent it is. Some rubbing trees have been used so much and for so long there are deep depressions in the ground. Some of the depressions result from bears stepping in the same places as they approach and leave the tree.

Turned-over rocks and logs are common sights in bear country. Both grizzlies and black bears turn over rocks and logs to look for insects. Photo B869 shows a freshly flipped tree trunk on the top of a ridge. It was probably done by a grizzly since we saw 12 grizzlies in the area that day.

Torn-up stumps and trees are another sign. Both grizzlies and black bears exhibit this behavior. In most cases they are looking for carpenter ants. Photo B865 shows a stump that was torn apart by a bear.

Bear tracks are one of the most exciting signs, especially if the tracks are very fresh. Photo T48 shows tracks of a presumably very large male grizzly in the snow. The human tracks are mine. The sole of my hiking boot is 12.5 inches long, so you have an idea of how large the bear track was. A very large bear made these tracks (see Chapter 11).

Probably the most important factor when discovering bear tracks is determining their age. Age is significant because it can indicate whether the bear is nearby. For example, one time I was hiking a trail as the snow was falling and there was about an inch of snow on the trail. I came across grizzly tracks. The first thing I noticed was that there were only a few flakes of snow in each track, even though it had been snowing steadily for 20 minutes. Obviously the bear was nearby. As I cautiously walked ahead a few yards, I noticed several trees had recently been rubbed. Then I detected an odor like that of a wet dog. The bear

B869

B865

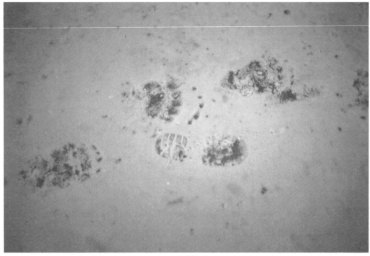

T48

was near, playing some kind of game with me. I turned around and left. I never saw the bear.

Because it was snowing, it had been easy to tell the age of the tracks. Other times it is not easy. Some of the most difficult conditions are dry and dusty trails. I have seen perfectly formed tracks on dusty trails one day and seen them again, looking just as perfect, the next day. Successfully determining the age of tracks comes with experience in the field. When in doubt, always assume the bear is nearby.

The most obvious difference between grizzly and black bear tracks is the distance from the front claw tips to the front toe pads. Many times you can't even see the claw tips on a front black bear track because the claws are so short, compared to a grizzly's claws.

The ability to identify and age bear sign is one of the most important aspects for hiking safely in bear country. Sign recognition must be an important component in anyone's hiking strategy.

CHAPTER 3

MAKING NOISE

Making the right noise in the right situation is probably the most important tactic for avoiding a bear encounter. It can also minimize the effects of an encounter. Conversely, making the wrong noise at the wrong time can make a situation much worse. In the following episodes notice when noise was made. Was it before the bear(s) were seen or after? Did the bear(s) know a human was there? What kind of noise was made? Was it loud or soft? What effect did it have?

JUNE, 1993
WEST SIDE, GLACIER NATIONAL PARK
I was hiking back from one of our observation points. It had been a beautiful warm, sunny day. Even though it was 8:45 pm., the sun was still rather high in the sky and the lighting was good. When I was about two-thirds of the way down the trail, I entered a wooded area. When I realized that visibility in the woods would be limited, I took out my bear spray. I carried it in my hand with the safety off. As I approached a blind turn in the trail, I slowed down and cautiously went around the corner.

As soon as I could see further down the trail, a small grizzly came out of the woods. I immediately stopped and watched it. The grizzly was about 40 yards in front of me when it stopped and looked back uphill into the woods. It appeared to be a two-year-old grizzly that was waiting for another bear. Jim Cole, a great friend and my close associate, had seen a pair of two-year-olds in the same vicinity a month earlier. I automatically assumed these were the same bears and started to reach for my camera. I thought I would take a picture of the two young bears when the other one reached the trail

All of a sudden a larger bear stepped out from the trees. It moved in front of the smaller bear and started up the trail towards me. At that moment I knew it was a female grizzly and her two-year-old cub, and they were totally unaware of my presence. I realized I had better make them aware really fast, before they got much closer. I didn't want to shout because I thought a shout, in that situation, might seem too alarming or threatening, so I loudly cleared my throat. The bears heard me instantly. The female stood up, eyed me for two seconds, spun around, and ran off. She crashed through the alders, heading downhill with the cub hot on her heels.

As I hiked past the spot where they had left the trail, I continued to make noise. I knew the bears had not been a threat, but I wanted them to know where I was in case they wandered close to the trail again. The trail turned back into the area where they had gone. However, I reached the trailhead about 35 minutes later without seeing any sign of them.

This was a classic encounter with a typical ending: the bears ran away.

JULY, 1993 WEST SIDE
Glacier National Park

This encounter occurred with the same bears as above, on the same trail. Only this time I was headed up to the observation point in the morning.

My original plan was to hike from Logan Pass to the observation point and return on a different trail. This plan required that I park my car at the lower trailhead and hitchhike to Logan Pass at the beginning of the upper trailhead. However, as I parked my car at the lower trailhead, I noticed a line of cars stopped on the road ahead of me. Apparently a snow bank had collapsed on the road, blocking it, and nobody knew for sure when the road would be reopened. As I sat near my car pondering my next move, a van of tourists stopped. They got out of their vehicle and started hiking up the trail towards my destination. I quickly gathered my gear and started up the trail. I knew there were bears higher up and I wanted to get there before all these people "invaded" the area.

I finally passed the group of about 15 people about halfway up the trail. I was sweating profusely and needed to re-hydrate, so I took a break. The group soon passed me. Once again I gathered my gear and raced towards them. I knew they would soon reach a prime area for bears. I passed them as they were about to reach an open

B1015

meadow, and as I arrived at the meadow, I was totally surprised to see a grizzly bear walking parallel to me about 40 feet away.

I stopped and grabbed my bear spray. The bear, digging glacier lily roots, was absolutely unconcerned with my presence. A two-year-old cub was behind it. They were the same bears that I had encountered on this trail in June. The cub seemed a little nervous (photo B1015) and stayed behind its mother, who appeared very calm. The group of people caught up to me and the female grizzly's reaction did not change. I started taking pictures.

The guide for the tourist group came forward and told the group they were watching a black bear mother and cub. I told her the bears were grizzlies.

Probably because of the number of people congregated so close, the bears slowly moved away until they finally disappeared into the cover. I continued to the observation point and finished the day by seeing three more grizzlies.

The female and her two-year-old cub acted quite differently from my previous encounter with them. They seemed more habituated to people. However, the time of day (it was getting lighter versus getting darker) could have been a factor in their behavior. The bear may have been accustomed to people on the trail at that time of day and would not have been as surprised. Also, there was a fair amount of noise coming from the people on the trail. Perhaps the bears heard us and knew we were approaching, instead of being surprised like my sudden appearance in June.

Many experts say that hiking in groups of four or more is usually very safe. This is because the noise generated by normal conversations within such groups is usually enough to alert a bear to approaching people and thus avoid surprises. Also, groups create a larger, more formidable presence, thus possibly deterring a bear from aggressive behavior.

In any case, the encounters ended as most encounters normally do: the bears left.

MAY 1996
West Side, Glacier National Park

My wife, Suzi, and I decided it would be a good day to make our annual pilgrimage to a series of avalanche chutes to look for grizzlies. Bears often forage on plants in the chutes and in the spring they also look for animals killed by winter avalanches. The Going to the Sun Road was still closed to vehicle traffic but open to hikers

B509

and bikers. It was an easy hike on the road, and as we approached the chutes we noticed how lush and green everything appeared.

Soon after we arrived we spotted two separate grizzlies high in the open areas. We continued to study the mountainsides for more grizzlies but without any luck. We decided to split up to cover more ground. Suzi was about 100 yards from me when I noticed a black bear meandering through the thick forest near the road. I grabbed my camera but the light was not good. I continued to watch the bear. The bear soon noted my presence, although it probably already knew we were there because of our talking earlier.

The bear walked towards the road and directly towards me. As soon as it emerged from the woods and into the good light, I began taking pictures. Now the bear's attention seemed intensely riveted on me (photo B509). I was beginning to wonder what the heck was going on. The bear came closer. I put away my camera and got out my bear spray. I really didn't want to spray this bear. The whole idea seemed ridiculous—spraying a black bear? But the bear seemed inexplicably drawn to me, like metal to a magnet. I wasn't really afraid. The bear was probably just curious. It seemed like it wanted to come up and smell me or touch me. I couldn't let that happen. That would be ludicrous and potentially dangerous.

My wife was totally unaware of what was happening to me. She was 100 yards down the road and in my direct line of sight, but she was looking in every direction except mine. In any case, I had to do something and do it fast. The bear was now only about 10 feet away.

I started hollering at the bear. I yelled, "GO ON! Get out of here! NO!" The bear stopped briefly, only five feet away, and then moved laterally to the other side of the road. My wife heard me and looked over, expecting to see me yelling at a dog because that's how I sound when I yell at our dogs when they're getting in trouble. She was quite humored to see me interacting that way with a black bear. I actually was a little embarrassed for letting the situation get to that point. I probably should have done something sooner to prevent the bear from getting that close. However, I was just as curious as the bear. I was trying to figure out what the bear was doing. The bear eventually disappeared into thick cover and we never saw it again.

This encounter was rather humorous. However, it did present some serious implications that I only realized later. Black bears that hang around or even deliberately approach a person may not be curious. They may be predatory. Although extremely rare, these kinds of bears must be dealt with immediately and sternly. The best way is to become aggressive, hollering and/or using some kind of aversive stimulus such as bear spray. In this case, I do not believe this particular bear was predatory, and I ended up utilizing the appropriate strategy. I just should have been done it sooner.

SEPTEMBER, 1997
West Side, Glacier National Park

I had spent the afternoon at Granite Park Chalet, talking to visitors and employees and surveying the area for grizzlies.

The huckleberries were in prime condition and rather plentiful, and people had been seeing grizzlies fairly often. In particular, hikers had seen a female grizzly and her two-year-old cubs quite regularly in the distance along the Loop Trail. A week earlier a companion and I had heard huffing from a berry patch close to the trail, but because of the thick cover we were unable to see the bears.

With all this in mind, I started hiking back to the road about 6 pm. As I was the last one down the trail, I was especially cautious and deliberate. I made noise and looked in all directions for any movement. About a half mile down the four-mile trail, I stopped at a small clearing at the edge of a steep embankment, where I could view some open areas. I was reaching for my binoculars when I heard a twig snap behind me.

I knew it was a grizzly and most likely the female with two-year-old cubs. I grabbed my bear spray and snapped the safety off. I looked in the direction of the noise and was dismayed to see that a small group of trees, 10 feet in front of me, totally obscured my vision. This was not good. I did not want the family group to walk through the trees and emerge at point blank range, so I cleared my throat. The response was quick and frightening. I heard a loud "huff" and then the sound of brush moving as the bear(s) approached. I had nowhere to go. To make matters worse, as I was peering through the trees to see if I could detect any movement, I was looking right into the sun, low in the western sky. The loud huffing continued. This really was not good. I actually felt scared and flirted with the idea that this could be it.

I stepped as far from the trees as possible, which wasn't very far, and strained for a glimpse of anything. Then I saw the bears. It was the female with her large cubs about 40 yards away, walking towards my right. All the bears were looking directly at me. They continued walking past the trees and disappeared.

"Whew!" I breathed a big sigh of relief. Not being able to see bears that you know are nearby and agitated by your presence is unnerving. Luckily these bears were familiar with people using the trail. I believe that stopping to glass probably prevented me from hiking right into them. I also believe that clearing my throat (making some noise that identified me as a human) also helped because it probably encouraged the female to detour around me. As I continued hiking, I saw evidence that she had been foraging on huckleberries 20 feet from the trail. This was a close call.

SEPTEMBER 1998
West Side, Glacier National Park

Joseph Brady, a hiking partner and bear enthusiast, and I went hiking to check on huckleberry production. We also hoped to observe grizzlies. We reached our destination and for the next three hours observed six grizzlies and at least 11 black bears searching for and eating any available berries. The area usually provided a reliable source of huckleberries but this year it was poor.

On the way out we hiked down a ridge. I was leading with Joseph about 15 yards behind me. Because it was densely wooded to our left, most of my attention was focused there. The area to our right was more open. As I do many times, I made coughing noises. I think coughing is a less intrusive way to make noise but still get a bear's attention. We carried our bear spray in our hands because we were in prime habitat. All of a sudden I became aware

B663

that Joseph was trying to get my attention. As I turned towards him, I saw the brush moving to my right and heard a crashing noise moving away from us. Joseph said it was a grizzly but I saw nothing. A few seconds later a black bear scurried up a snag (photo B663) near the crashing noise. Apparently the escaping grizzly had scared the black bear up the tree.

After we stood still for a while, the crashing noise ended, and the black bear climbed down. Joseph explained what happened. As I was directing my attention towards my left, Joseph noticed a grizzly watching me about 40 yards to my right. Because I had been coughing to make noise, I hadn't heard the grizzly's huffing or Joseph's repeated attempts to get my attention. I believe the grizzly finally ran because it became unsettled that I ignored it and kept walking. It may also have heard Joseph's raised voice when he called to me. In any event, the bear certainly did not act habituated.

I believe my hiking strategy was correct under the circumstances. The wooded area posed the greatest risk because the cover was dense and close. The more open, right side provided us (and a bear) with more room to react and therefore more options. My coughing probably got the bear's attention even though I had been trying to direct the noise towards the woods, so I don't believe the bear was totally surprised. If the bear would have made a move towards me, Joseph would have yelled louder, and I would have had time to turn and act appropriately.

APRIL, 1999
Going to the Sun Road, Glacier National Park

I was hiking on the Going to the Sun Road before it was open to vehicles. About a mile west of Avalanche Creek Campground I noticed something dark on a roadside snow bank about 50 yards ahead. I stopped and was surprised to see it was a grizzly. I often wonder how close the bear would have let me approach before it indicated it was there.

B781

The moment I stopped, the bear got up and approached (photo B781). I remained calm as the bear walked towards me. It was a black-colored grizzly and appeared young, perhaps three or four years old. It was one of the most unique and beautiful bears I had ever seen. As it kept approaching, and because it did not appear to be agitated or aggressive, I decided to experiment. I wanted to know, if possible, what gestures or sounds would halt a bear's advance without spooking it.

B772

I put my hands in the air to make myself look bigger. The bear kept coming. I turned sideways (I was wearing a large pack) and put my hands in the air to make myself look bigger and more imposing. The bear kept coming. I turned and faced the bear and said in a calm, soothing voice, "Oh what a good bear - Oh what a pretty bear," as if I were talking to a dog. The bear stopped as I spoke. When I stopped talking, the bear continued towards me. When I again started talking in the same tone of voice, the bear stopped.

B786

33

I stopped talking, and the bear started walking towards me. It was now less than 30 yards away and moving from the right side of the road to the left (photo B772). I moved towards the right side of the road. The bear climbed onto a snow bank on the left side. To maintain level eye contact, I climbed onto a snow bank on the right side. The bear jumped off the snow bank (photo B786) and moved towards me. It was less than 20 yards away. I wanted to stay at the level of the bear and I wanted to stay on the pavement because it offered better footing, so I jumped off my snow bank towards the bear. The instant I jumped onto the road, the bear ran in the opposite direction.

This encounter was very informative. I believe the bear was merely curious. That is why it approached. It was also a young bear and might have been testing me. In either situation, I believe holding your ground is very important. If I had backed away, the bear probably would have followed. It might have seen backing up as a sign of weakness, leading to an attempt to dominate and test me, with unknown consequences for me and the bear. That's why I tried to remain at the same level as the bear and maintain eye contact. I did not want the bear to think it was getting the upper hand or dominating me. When I jumped towards it, the bear realized it could not dominate me and possibly thought I was dominant. That is most likely why it ran. However, jumping is a quick movement that I think should only be used in special circumstances. As a matter of fact, this was the first time I ever made a quick movement towards a bear.

It is important to note that my voice was enough to stop the bear as it approached. *I believe a non-threatening vocalization may be one of the best ways to stop an approaching bear.* This has worked for me on other occasions.

OCTOBER, 1999
East Side, Glacier National Park

On a windy, overcast, but fairly mild October day I was hiking from the east side of the park up and over the Continental Divide to the west side and back again. I was fond of this route because it covered major grizzly habitat throughout the hike.

At the start of the final climb up the pass, I noticed an extensive patch of ripe and firm huckleberries. I proceeded through the area, alert and making noise. I made a mental note to be extra alert and cautious in this area on the way back. I reached the west side of the pass and in the distance saw a grizzly digging glacier lily roots. After examining the area for a while and seeing nothing else, I headed back.

As I entered the huckleberry patch I had noted earlier, I stopped and scanned the area in great detail. I felt that I should yell as loud as possible before I moved on. The wind was howling, which would muffle any noise, so I gave my best holler, a loud "YOOOÖ!" To my surprise, a smallish grizzly appeared below me. It emerged right at the base of the pass next to the trail. I grabbed my camera and took a photo. Then I noticed another yearling cub and its mother coming out of the thick brush. They were about 100 yards directly below me (photo B1016) and well aware of my presence, thanks to my hollering. They kept an eye on me as they moved away from the trail into the opening. I stood still and watched them as they retreated. They did not run but moved at a steady pace. They crossed a small, bare knoll and then went up the opposite side of the drainage. When they were a safe distance away, I continued hiking, keeping an eye out for them. I finally rounded a corner and lost sight of them. I saw two more grizzlies eating huckleberries on my way out.

B1016

Yelling really paid off. If I had not yelled, I probably would have run into these bears at a very close distance. I may even have provoked a charge, as it would have been a surprise encounter.

I yelled because I was approaching a prime food source, I could not see very well because of the brush, and the wind was muffling the trail coughing that I normally do. Awareness of these conditions dictated the hiking strategy.

OCTOBER, 2000
Nyack-Coal Creek Loop, Glacier National Park

This 45-mile, 3-day hike took place in one of the most remote areas in Glacier. The area is rarely visited, for good reason. The trails are normally very wet and sometimes hard to find. Hikers must ford creeks and rivers 11 times. If something goes wrong, it's a long way from help. This is also prime grizzly country. I took the hike because I had never been in the area and I wanted to check the habitat and look for grizzly sign.

I crossed the Middle Fork of the Flathead River and began to notice quite a few fresh grizzly tracks on the trail. Fresh tracks and fresh scat would be common the rest of the hike. Since I was hiking alone, I carried my bear spray with the safety off for much of the three days. I also made quite a bit of noise: coughing or yelling where and when I felt it was appropriate.

The first night I set up camp at the Upper Nyack Campground near Nyack Creek, below the north face of Mount Stimson. It was eerily beautiful. I was the only one in camp. In fact, I never saw another soul during the entire trek. I built a small fire in the fire pit at the food area, which was about 100 yards from my campsite. The fire did not last long. The wood was too damp. I ate my supper of dried food. I do not like to cook in prime grizzly habitat because of possible odors that might attract a bear. I suspended my food bag on the line provided at the food area and went back to my tent. It was now dark.

Suffice it to say, I did not sleep very well. Any noise caused me to stir. I kept a can of bear spray in my sleeping bag for accessibility. I kept another can of bear spray outside of my sleeping bag next to my shoulder. I awoke at about 8 am. The temperature had dipped to 10 degrees. My boots and hiking pants, wet from the previous day's hiking, were frozen solid. It took me awhile to get my boots on because they were so stiff. I went down to the creek to filter water, came back and broke camp. It was about 9:40 am.

After hiking for a little less than an hour, I approached Pacific Creek. I looked up and saw a grizzly on the trail on the other side of the creek. It was about 20 yards east of the creek. I was about 20 yards west of the creek. The bear was not aware of me. It had just rounded a blind curve on the trail and had probably not heard the noise I had been making. I froze and said "Hello" in a calm voice but loud enough so the bear would hear me over the noise of the creek.

The bear immediately stopped. We studied each other. I said, "Oh what a good bear, Oh what a pretty bear," in a calm, soothing voice. The bear really did not look like it wanted to leave the trail to bushwhack around me. I did not want to bushwhack around the bear, nor did I want to turn around and go back, although that was an option. I wanted to continue in the direction I had been hiking and the bear looked as if it wanted to go in the direction it had been walking—towards me.

After standing on all fours for about 30 seconds, the bear slowly started to turn around, still looking at me to see if I might change my mind and leave the trail so it could continue on. I held my ground. The bear disappeared up the trail around the blind curve. Now I had a new dilemma. I was hiking in that direction, but now I knew there was a grizzly ahead on the trail and I could not see it or know its exact whereabouts. I ended up staying in the same spot on the trail while I talked loudly to myself. I figured the bear would leave the trail and bushwhack around me or keep traveling up the trail away from me.

After waiting 10 to 15 minutes, I walked up the trail, talking loudly. I rounded the blind curve very deliberately, holding my bear spray with the safety off. After I hiked another 100 yards, I saw the bear's tracks where it had moved off the trail to go around me.

I made it to the Coal Creek Campground around dusk, which was much later than I intended. (The mileage on the trail signs was not accurate.) This could have been dangerous, since I had seen fresh grizzly scat along the last five miles of trail. In very poor light, I set up camp in the only campsite I could find. The food area was only about 30 yards from my tent. This was entirely too close for comfort, especially when one is that isolated. I hung my food bag on the line provided and went to bed. Once again, I slept restlessly. And once again, my boots and pants were frozen in the morning. I finished the hike later that day without incident.

I believe this adventure provides many key points. The first important point is proper hiking behavior when alone. No one recommends traveling in grizzly country alone. In fact, hiking alone is not recommended in any situation. The risks are rather obvious, including getting injured without being able to obtain help. However, if you are experienced, knowledgeable, understand the risks, and use common sense, the risks can be managed.

Second, camping sites, food, and odors are very important. I don't like camping near creeks because of the noise they produce and because bears commonly use creek bottoms for travel. However, one may not have a choice on the campsites. Many of the designated campgrounds in Glacier National Park are near prime grizzly travel corridors. This makes food and odor management even more important. I store food properly and try to reduce food odors as much as possible. Carrying only dry food and cooking only when necessary (during extended outings) are the best precautions.

Third, the encounter with the grizzly once again shows the importance of remaining calm and refraining from sudden movements. I believe my tone of voice helped convince the bear that I was not a threat. I think the bear concluded that I was, at most, an inconvenience. It appeared to be an average-sized grizzly. It might have been a younger bear, perhaps four or five years old, but I wasn't sure. If it had been a larger bear, it might have tried to intimidate me or dominate me off the trail, or it might have run away immediately because large male bears usually avoid humans at every opportunity (See Chapter 11). In any case, I believe I carried out the correct encounter strategy for this particular situation.

NOVEMBER, 2001
West Side, Glacier National Park

In November I usually hike at lower elevations where there is less snow and more available bear food. I was hiking around and through open meadows, looking for grizzly diggings. At one particular meadow I discovered a significant amount of what appeared to be clover root scat. The scat was of varying diameters, and I felt the diameter differences were attributable to the amounts eaten.

After hiking through the meadow a number of times, I exited onto a tight trail that went through a dense grove of 12-year-old lodgepole pines. I was very alert, making coughing sounds, and had my bear spray out and ready the whole time. There was fairly fresh scat on the trail. I reached a dirt road that led back to my vehicle. However, before I continued, I stopped at a steep bluff overlooking a river to check some open areas on the other side of the river. I heard small rocks and gravel falling down a steep bank near me, about 30 feet away. It had begun to rain and I figured the gravel was being loosened by the rain and didn't give it a second thought.

I turned around and walked about 30 feet to the road. All of a sudden I heard a loud "huff," snapping branches, and crashing sounds coming right at me. I ran to the other side of the road. I have said never run during a bear encounter. Well, I needed additional open space between myself and the dense stand of pines. I already had my bear spray out. I only needed room to use it.

It only took me a few strides to reach the other side of the road. Then I turned around to face the noise and said in a calm voice, "Oh what a good bear you are." The crashing sounds immediately stopped. I waited a few seconds and slowly continued down the road towards my truck. I strained to look through the trees for a glimpse of the bear.

After about 50 yards I saw it. It appeared rather small and very calm. It looked like it was just sitting on the edge of the bank. I realized that if I could get to my truck I could drive to the other side of the river for a better view. I reached my truck, drove to the other side and got out. Looking back at the steep bank, I couldn't believe what I saw. Not more than 30 feet from where I had been standing, where the gravel had been rolling down the bank, was a female grizzly and two yearling cubs. Wow, I had guessed wrong on a lot of things!

The rain wasn't rolling the gravel. It was the bears, digging hedysarum roots. It obviously wasn't the smallish single bear on top of the steep bank that charged me but the adult female protecting her cubs. And the diameter of the scat varied because it was coming from different sized bears—duh.

Whoever thought I knew what I was doing? Some days you just guess wrong, and guessing wrong may have serious consequences for you and the bear. At least I felt I reacted to the encounter in the appropriate manner. I had my bear spray ready. I remained calm. I spoke in calm, soothing voice that elicited the right response from the bear. My assumptions were wrong, but my encounter strategy worked, especially the sound of my voice.

CHAPTER 4
RECOGNIZING BEAR SIGN

Bear sign indicates that bears have been there, may still be nearby, and may come back. In many situations, finding bear sign has caused me to change my hiking strategy. Of course, the absence of bear sign does not guarantee the absence of bears.

JULY, 1996
West Side, Glacier National Park

At 5:30 in the morning, Jim Cole and I began a 24-mile day hike on the west side of Glacier. It was an absolutely beautiful, dry morning. About 8 am we approached a promising, open meadow. As soon as we began to explore, we discovered fresh diggings of glacier lily roots. From that evidence, we knew a grizzly was somewhere nearby. Slowly and carefully we hiked through the meadow, which was broken by small groups of trees. Fresh diggings were everywhere, so we had our cans of bear spray out and ready. We were especially cautious near the trees because of the limited visibility.

Two small groups of trees were on either side of us. Suddenly we heard a loud "huff." About 35 yards away we saw a grizzly standing on its hind feet looking right at us. A little cub-of-the-year was next to it. I thought about reaching for my camera. The light was perfect, and a bear's standing position, in most cases, is not a sign of aggression but rather a way in which a bear gets a better look or smell. However, a bear can come out of a standing position in any number of ways, and I knew the mother grizzly could certainly come down and charge. So we froze, remained calm, and watched the female's reaction to us.

She came down on all four paws, swung her body around, and ran in the opposite direction. The cub was tight on her heels. We never like to spook bears but it happens once in a while. As happens in most encounters, cubs or no cubs, the bears ran away.

SEPTEMBER, 1998
East Side, Glacier National Park

Joseph Brady and I got an early start on a clear, beautiful, autumn day. The first few miles of the hike went without incident. We were hiking to an area that was mostly above tree line. It was visible from the road, and from the road with binoculars we had previously seen grizzlies in the vicinity.

B1025

B1026

As we came out of the forest into an opening, we saw fresh grizzly tracks in the snow. The tracks indicated a female with at least one cub-of-the-year. We proceeded cautiously with our bear spray ready. We felt safe since we were in the open and had good visibility in all directions. We hiked very slowly and stopped often to listen and scan the immediate area. Grizzlies by nature are fairly noisy. They don't sneak around like mountain lions. You can hear them moving through the brush or digging roots.

As we rounded a slight curve in the trail, we entered an area that had been out of sight. About 70 yards down the mountainside we saw a female grizzly and two cubs-of-the-year. They were digging and did not notice us. We froze and remained calm. I reached for my

B1024

camera and began taking pictures. The female must have heard the shutter or caught our scent. In any case she looked directly at us, hesitated for a second, and then turned and ran for the closest cover with her cubs in pursuit (photos B1025, B1026, B1024).

Once again this short encounter ended with the most predictable result—the bears ran away. The bears did not feel boxed in. They had plenty of escape routes and protective cover was close. Also, we made no sudden movements or threatening noises. In other words, the female bear did not perceive us as a threat that needed to be dealt with in any other way than by running away. We continued our hike and saw two single grizzlies further up the trail. They also were digging roots.

OCTOBER, 2000
Whitefish Range, Flathead National Forest

This story is about a bear encounter that was avoided. Obviously such events are hard to document because you don't see the bear you don't encounter.

On this hike I hoped to observe grizzly utilization of glacier lily roots and/or huckleberries. The trail followed a high ridgeline for about half the distance. Just before it dropped into a wooded area, there was an observation point that I used to view some open, rocky benches. After a half hour without seeing anything, I hiked to the area. It took about an hour to reach it. I saw only old diggings, probably from the summer. I walked around for another 15 minutes when I suddenly spotted fresh—"smoking fresh"—diggings of glacier lily roots. I knew a bear was close by. In fact, I may have already, unintentionally, spooked it. I had been hiking with my bear spray out and the safety off. I knew this was prime grizzly habitat and a bear encounter could occur at any moment. I retreated, not by the way I came in but by a more direct route to the trail. I continued to see fresh diggings. I felt that the bear may have heard me and moved away. However, I was still alert. I took nothing for granted.

I returned to my observation point and started glassing the rocky area again. Within 100 yards of where I first saw the fresh diggings, I spotted a grizzly bear, busily digging. I set up my spotting scope and watched the bear intensely for about 45 minutes. When I was in that area, I must have been very close to the bear. I had not yelled because I did not want to spook any bears or change their behavior. Noise at the wrong time can create a surprise or a threat where none existed in the first place. I don't know if the bear ever knew I was in the area. In any event, it appeared the bear's behavior was not changed in any way.

This "non-encounter" is an example of how proper identification of bear sign and food sources should affect your hiking strategy, resulting in a positive outcome for both the hiker and the bear. Recognizing fresh bear sign allows you to leave an area where a bear is present, thereby decreasing the chances of an encounter or of spooking the bear. The more you know about grizzly habitat, sign, and behavior, the better you will be able to devise effective strategies for hiking and for personal responses.

CHAPTER 5
REMAIN STILL & CALM

*P*robably the single most important action to take when a bear is encountered is to freeze and remain still and calm while watching the bear's reaction to your presence. I have learned that in order to make the right decisions in bear encounters, you must first determine if the bear reacts negatively to you or your group. The bear's reaction will then determine what you do next, what I call your "personal response strategy." Remaining still and calm during this initial process"helps you act more rationally and may help the bear decide that you are not a threat. In addition, remaining still (holding your ground) even in cases where the bear moves towards you sometimes indicates to the bear that you cannot be intimidated.

AUGUST, 1992
West Side, Glacier National Park

Jim Cole and I took a hike on the west side of Glacier to explore new country. We started very early in the morning to reach a good viewing location along a high ridge by sunrise. Much of the hike was off trail. Huckleberry bushes were just starting to turn red, and as the sun rose on the ridge, their brilliant colors became evident. We felt we had a good chance to see a grizzly or two that day, especially since the "hucks" were ripe all the way to the top of the ridgeline.

We came to the edge of a small side canyon that cut into the ridge. I was leading when we started down the steep embankment towards the bottom of the canyon. In the thick cover below and to our left, we suddenly heard an incredible thrashing and crashing. Of course our first thought was a grizzly, but we saw a huge bull moose running away from us, crashing through the alders and huckleberry bushes. We decided we had probably spooked the moose, but we were aware a grizzly also could have scared it.

I continued down the steep bank with my bear spray in hand and the safety off. As I reached the very bottom of the cut, I heard a huffing sound and it was getting closer. The sound was like an approaching steam locomotive, and it was coming from the area where the moose had been spooked. This time we knew it was a grizzly. I stood my ground at the bottom of the narrow canyon and faced the sound. Jim remained still on the side of the embankment. I remained calm with my bear spray in my outstretched hand, pointing at the direction of the huffing. There was nothing else to do but wait. We didn't want to make noise because we could tell the bear was already stressed.

The grizzly tore out of the brush on a straight run about 40 yards in front of me. When it saw me it did not break stride but turned to its left and continued into the thick brush. There was still a huffing sound coming from the same area. It was another bear. I remained still while the second grizzly came into the open. This bear was larger, and when it saw me, it stopped dead in its tracks and took what seemed like a good long look at me. Then it followed the slightly smaller bear into the thick brush and disappeared. For a second I thought the second bear might charge after it stopped. However, having the option of using the bear spray, which I had ready, I did not feel threatened or scared.

In a few seconds everything was still. Jim came down and we immediately started up the other side of the cut. We did not feel safe at the bottom of the small canyon. When we reached the top on the other side, we discussed what had just happened. We both realized we had encountered a female grizzly with a two-year-old cub. The bears either spooked the moose or visa versa, or we spooked the moose and the moose spooked them. The fact that the mother was behind the cub indicated that the threat she perceived was behind them and not in front of them where we were. In any case they wanted to get to a new area really fast. Unfortunately, I was in their way.

In this encounter, I felt both Jim and I did the right thing. Actually, I'm not aware of any other alternatives. The event reinforced my main concept of freezing and remaining calm as the important first act in a bear encounter.

MAY, 1994
South Side, Glacier National Park

Jim and I decided to make two hikes in one day on the south side of Glacier. We reached the first trailhead in the early morning. Our objective was a nearby mountain to check on abundant glacier lilies there. We reached the summit without seeing any bears. On the way down we bushwhacked off trail. About halfway down we spotted a black bear at the bottom of an avalanche chute. After viewing this bear, we descended without seeing any other bears.

For our afternoon hike our ultimate destination was a place where we had seen a large male grizzly the previous spring. We planned to pass the bottom of the same avalanche chute where we had seen the black bear earlier in the day. As we approached the chute we were quiet but cautious and alert. The moment we reached the edge of the chute, where we could see to the bottom of it, we spotted what we assumed was the same black bear. We were much lower and therefore much closer than we had been earlier. We studied the bear for a while, trying to determine what it was eating. Then we continued into the chute. We noticed it was filled with bright yellow glacier lilies and thick willows and alders. Our goal, however, was to explore a biscuitroot hillside another mile up the trail.

Jim was in the lead when we reached the other side of the chute. I was looking down, watching my footing, when all of a sudden Jim said, "Tim—there is a large grizzly right in front of us on the trail." The grizzly was about 40 yards away. Of course we both froze in our tracks. I had been carrying my bear spray with the safety off because of the thick cover in the chute. The bear looked at us, moved off the trail, and circled above us. He traveled to a small knob about 35 yards away. By this time Jim and I had our cameras out.

B285

47

The bear stopped, stood up, and looked at us (photo B285). The bear did not seem accustomed to humans. However, he seemed to have the attitude that we were not going to intimidate him in his territory. He simply came down and slowly ambled off in the opposite direction from where we were going.

We continued hiking without seeing another bear. On the way back we made plenty of noise to make sure that we did not run into the large grizzly again.

One vitally important aspect when hiking is to never lose sight of the bigger picture. We spent a lot of time that day concentrating, for whatever reason, on one black bear to the exclusion of what we were really looking for—grizzlies. We may have let our guard down by thinking that a black bear would not be so calm if a grizzly was nearby. Well, that theory proved wrong. Anything is possible, and hikers should be adequately prepared when it comes to the behavior of bears.

Our hiking strategy was valid. I had the bear spray out, but I would have had it out in any case because of the thick cover. Being in a state of high alert whenever you travel through thick cover cannot be emphasized enough. In any case, things worked out, as in most encounters. The bear left without incident, albeit not in the normal fashion (i.e. running). Our encounter strategy was also valid. We froze and watched the bear's reaction to us. The bear's reaction dictated that we could think about taking pictures.

SEPTEMBER, 1996
West Side, Glacier National Park

Jim Cole and I took a day hike to check various areas between 6000 and 7000 feet for huckleberries. As we approached 5,500 feet, ripe huckleberries appeared on the bushes. As we approached 6000 feet, the berries became abundant. It looked like a good day for spotting grizzlies.

We arrived at our main lookout and immediately saw grizzlies below us and at a distance, foraging on huckleberries. We observed their behavior for some time and decided to check other areas. We spotted a female grizzly and yearling cub foraging on huckleberries, watched them for a while, and then went back to our main lookout.

As we were approaching the lookout, we saw a female grizzly and two yearlings running away from us into the trees. When we got closer to our observation area, we ran into this same family group again. At this point we were about 40 yards away. We immediately froze, remained calm, and watched how the bears reacted to us. The cubs immediately ran in the opposite direction and disappeared behind a group of trees. The female held her ground between us and her cubs and watched our reaction to her (photo B463). She looked towards the cubs, then looked back at us. Upon realizing we were not a threat, she turned and ran after her cubs.

B463

Once again we had an encounter that ended with the bears running away. However, this situation could have been far different if we had reacted in a different manner. For example, if we had started hollering or waving our arms in the air, rather than remaining still and calm, the mother might have perceived us as a threat and charged. Of course, if the cubs had been between us and her, or, in the worst-case scenario, if we had been between her and her cubs, the situation definitely would have been more challenging.

APRIL, 2000
Going to the Sun Road, Glacier National Park

It was a beautiful, warm, sunny spring day and I was biking on the Going to the Sun Road. I started where the gate closed the road to vehicles near the head of Lake McDonald. Many cars were in the parking area; a lot of people had the same idea.

About 1.5 miles into my journey I looked up and saw a grizzly about 100 yards ahead of me, walking towards me on the road. No

B798

B799

B800

B801

one else was around. I got off my bike and started taking photos (photos B798 and B799). The bear was aware of my presence but kept coming. As it approached, it moved to the creek side of the road. It looked as if it would come within 10 yards of me, or closer, if I did not move. When it was about 35 yards away and still approaching, I turned my bike sideways in front of me. The bear immediately changed direction, headed for the opposite side of the road, and disappeared into heavy cover (photos B800 and B801). I never saw it again.

It was a radio-collared bear and probably somewhat habituated. It had probably just moved down from its winter den and was on its way to a snow-free area. The road was the easiest way to travel, allowing the bear to conserve energy. As I learned later, many people saw the bear on the road.

It probably would have passed me on the road if I had not changed position. However, that was a risk I was not going to take without sending some message to the bear. Moving my bike in front of me while standing my ground provided some minimal protection and probably sent the bear a message. The bear either saw that movement as a sign of dominance or as an unknown situation that experience had not yet taught it how to handle. Another possibility was that the bear always reacted that way with people that turned their bike sideways. In any case, the bear did not become agitated or aggressive. It just changed its route.

CHAPTER 6
STAY TOGETHER

When hiking in a group (defined as two or more people), it is important to stay together. This is important not only in grizzly country but in any hiking situation. How many times have we heard of people getting lost after they became separated from their group? In grizzly country, staying together is important for many reasons. If people are spread out when they encounter a bear, the bear might feel it is being surrounded and therefore threatened. If people stay together, they form a more imposing presence to help dissuade a bear thinking of aggressive action. For just this reason, officials in many areas recommend hiking in groups of four or more people. Also, the noise generated by a large group's normal talking is usually enough to warn a bear of their approach and thereby avoid a surprise encounter.

SEPTEMBER 1998
Highline Trail, Glacier National Park

The Highline Trail is one of the most scenic hiking trails in the world, heavily used by hikers. It also happens to transverse some of the best grizzly habitat in North America.

About five miles into the hike Joseph and I met two hikers coming from the opposite direction. They said they had passed a grizzly near the trail about a mile back. They said the bear did not appear aggressive and it had not moved. In order to pass the bear, the hikers had to leave the trail and hike below it. We thanked them for the information and continued hiking. Most of the area along the trail is open and visibility is excellent. We continually scanned ahead, hoping to spot the bear from a distance. After rounding a bend, we saw the bear about 500 yards away, digging about 50 yards above the trail. We continued hiking as we kept our eyes on the bear.

As we came within 200 yards of the bear, we ran into a young Japanese man who was photographing bighorn sheep. He appar-

B627

B624

B631

ently did not notice the grizzly. We continued until we were about 100 yards from the bear. It was now only about 20 yards above the trail, so we hiked below the trail and stopped about 50 yards away. The bear had noticed us but did not move. It had a serious look on its face (photo B627) as if to say, don't come any closer. We stood still, remained calm, and took photos as the bear dug and ate hedysarum roots.

We noticed the young Japanese man approaching us on the trail. We motioned for him to quietly and slowly come over to us. When he got to us we told him to stay still, quiet, and not move. We continued studying the bear's behavior. It did not show any signs of agitation or aggression. I took a few more photos. As I was looking through my viewfinder, I noticed the bear's demeanor suddenly change. It swung its head around (photo B624) and looked to our left. Then it turned its whole body to face that direction (photo B631). Joseph and I wondered what was going on. Why was the bear acting that way? Then we saw the reason. While our attention was on the bear, the young hiker had walked away from us! We were shocked!

The bear started to huff and puff, inflating itself up, and began to act very agitated. From the bear's point-of-view, a non-threatening situation had now turned into a threatening one. It was being encircled. The bear looked like it was getting ready to charge the young man, who was about 40 yards from us. We yelled, "FREEZE!" The hiker stopped. Our yell also distracted the bear. It looked at us. We were again calm and quiet. It looked back at the young hiker. He was now still and quiet. The bear calmed down and went back to digging. When the bear's head was down, we quietly told the kid to slowly walk back to us, which he did. When he got back he was shaking. He said he was really scared. I'm sure he was very aware of what almost happened.

Because of the bear's reaction to the young man, we decided that following the same route might agitate the grizzly again. So we backtracked down the trail and then quietly bushwhacked around the grizzly far above it, high on the mountainside, the whole time keeping the bear in sight. The grizzly kept digging and eating roots. When we last saw the bear, it was still just above the trail.

A couple of good lessons can be learned from this encounter. First, it is important to remain calm and remain together. Never approach a bear or surround it. A relatively safe situation can quickly change to a dangerous encounter by a seemingly harmless action. Second, be prepared to change your hiking plans. If a bear's behavior changes, you must consider other options.

SEPTEMBER, 1998
Logan Pass, Glacier National Park

Joseph and I went to the Logan Pass Visitor Center to report grizzly activity we had observed on a hike. While we were outside talking to a ranger, we saw a lone grizzly in the distance, digging what appeared to be glacier lily roots. As we were relating the events of our hike, the bear moved closer and closer. I started taking photos. Soon everyone in the vicinity was watching the bear.

The bear approached within 20 yards of us and about 30 people who were standing next to us. People coming back to the visitor center on the Hidden Lake Trail had to stop because the bear was too close to the trail. Now

B644

B636

there were about 30 people on the other side of the bear. The bear was so close that I could see voles scared up by its digging. The bear would flatten a vole with a paw and then eat it (photo B644). The bear was getting a balanced meal. The ranger appeared rather nervous, trying to figure out how to handle the situation. This was a decent-sized adult grizzly, probably a male. There was really nothing the ranger could do.

The two groups of people remained calm and together. Nobody tried to approach the bear. Everyone, including the bear, was well behaved. This bear walked between the two groups, pretending not to notice our presence. The grizzly never looked at anyone. It was probably habituated. The bear continued feeding and disappeared into the distance (photo B636).

I do not believe the bear was staying near the visitor center for security from larger bears, but rather for the abundant food supply there. Many times we have observed grizzlies digging in the vast meadows surrounding the visitor center. However, we had never observed one this close.

In this situation, everyone stayed calm and stayed together, and the encounter had a good ending for everyone. For most people it was the grizzly sighting of a lifetime.

SEPTEMBER 1999
West Side, Glacier National Park

Jim Cole, Jim's brother Beau Grant, Steve Merlino, and I took a 12-mile hike to observe grizzly utilization of huckleberries. On our way back down we decided to stop on a ridge and take one last break and make one more viewing attempt. We had already seen 11 grizzlies that day, so we were very alert. As we were finishing our break, Steve said rather loudly, "Bear!"

My first reaction, before even looking up, was to grab my bear spray. About 20 yards away a grizzly approached us on the ridge. It appeared to be two or three years old. When I realized it was a young bear, I grabbed my camera and took a few rather hurried photos (photos B777 and B778). I snapped the photos as the bear went below us and to our left. It came within 10 yards and then continued into thick cover. We never saw this bear again.

B777

I felt this bear approached us because it was curious. I don't believe it intended to dominate us or that it was habituated. There were four of us, which was probably intimidating. If we had made any sudden movements, we probably would have spooked it. As it was, we stayed together, remained calm and still, and just watched.

B778

AUGUST 2001
East Side, Glacier National Park

Jim Cole and I met three wildlife photographers on the trail. We stopped to discuss the latest grizzly sightings and decided to hike up the trail together. Five sets of eyes were better than two.

We soon met two hikers who said they had seen a grizzly further up the trail. They were not very confident of its exact location, since they were not very familiar with the area. A little farther up the trail we met a group of 10 people all hurrying towards us. They emphatically and nervously stated that a grizzly was "stalking" them and they immediately continued down the trail. Jim and I looked at each other and started laughing. We knew it was probably a habituated grizzly walking on the trail because it's easier than walking through the heavy cover. We continued up the trail slowly and very alert. I had my bear spray ready. We were not assuming anything. We made noise by talking back and forth.

B829

B830

B831

I came to a bend in the trail, looked ahead and was shocked to see the grizzly right on the trail ahead of me. From its body size and shape, it looked like a young bear. I took a quick picture (photo B829). I was close and had no time to focus properly. In reality, I was too close to be taking photos. However, since the five of us formed an imposing group, I did not think this young bear was a threat. In addition, I realized this was a bear we had observed previously near the trail and it had never shown any sign of aggression. Indeed, it was rather habituated.

Nevertheless, we backed up and gave the bear room. It continued moving towards us as it crossed back and forth across the trail (photo B830), checking for berries. It finally moved uphill (photo B831). It continued looking for suitable berries as it moved up the mountain and out of photographic range.

I would never recommend taking the actions that I did during this encounter. Taking the quick photos when we first encountered the bear was not worth the risk. The photos didn't even turn out well but they do show the bear's reaction to a close encounter. Because of the group's size and my "knowing" this bear, I felt safe. To any objective observer, however, I probably looked like a complete idiot.

Keeping bears in sight until you can safely move away or until the bears have moved away is one of best things hikers can do. This is a mother grizzly and yearling cub in Glacier National Park.

CHAPTER 7
KEEP YOUR EYES ON THE BEAR

Being able to make the right decision to avoid an encounter (where a bear is seen at a distance, for example) or to safely survive an encounter depends in most cases of knowing exactly where the bear is. Even though large, a grizzly bear is adept at disappearing into its surroundings. Notice in the following situations the importance of keeping one's eyes on the bear.

AUGUST, 1992
West Side Glacier National Park

It was a very unusual late August day. A freak snowstorm had dumped a foot of snow in the area where Jim Cole and I were hiking. The huckleberries were just beginning to ripen over a wide area. As we gained elevation towards our destination, we were surprised to see numerous bear tracks in the snow. The tracks were heading up the trail in front of us. First we saw black bear tracks, and as we got even higher, we began to see grizzly tracks. The tracks were made by more than just a couple of bears.

Over the years Jim and I have located many observation spots throughout the ecosystems we have studied. One of the first such lookouts was our destination on this hike. From this cliff we had seen grizzlies digging glacier lily roots in the spring and eating huckleberries in the fall. On this particular day we were about to see an amazing display of bear behavior. We would see a total of 13 black bears and 8 grizzlies. All of the bears were eating huckleberries. Everywhere we looked we saw bears. The bears seemed to be aware that after a snow, berries turn to mush and fall off within a few days. The bears came "out of the woodwork" to eat as many berries as possible before there were no more to eat.

B271

B802

Of all the bears we saw that day, there were two that particularly intrigued us, a female grizzly and what appeared to be either a two-year-old cub or a rather large yearling. We first spotted these bears eating "hucks" about 250 yards below us. We continued to observe them as they came within 50 yards of us right below the cliff (photo B271). They were not aware of our presence. That is one of the reasons why we use this particular spot so much: bears rarely know we are there. Right after I took the photograph, the two bears seemed to disappear into thin air. One minute they were right below us and the next minute they were gone. We spent the next five minutes walking along the edge of the cliff hoping to spot them again, but without success. I finally turned and looked behind us and there they were (photo B802), lying down watching us. They were probably wondering, "What are those two dim wits doing over there?"

Somehow the bears had found a slot in the cliff, climbed up and circled around behind us without our being aware of their movements. This is an important example of why you should never take your eyes off a grizzly until you can safely leave the area. If you lose sight of a bear, you never know where it is likely to turn up. You could end up running right back into it. The fact that the bears lay down and watched us speaks volumes about their incredible curiosity and intelligence.

AUGUST, 1992
Great Bear Wilderness

Jim and I decided to explore a new area in the Great Bear Wilderness, which lies just south of Glacier National Park. From a distance I had previously seen grizzlies on a ridge in the area. On this hike we were going to hike directly into the ridge area.

It was a beautiful sunny day right before Labor Day weekend. As we climbed in elevation, the views were fantastic. We could see a beautiful crystal clear lake below us and towering mountains with hanging glaciers all around us. We reached the first saddle in a high ridge and bushwhacked along the ridge until we found a good observation point. We sat down and began viewing the open slopes around us. We ended up spotting four black bears over two hours. The bears appeared to be eating huckleberries and mountain ash. We backtracked to the first saddle and then continued on the loop trail.

We hiked through a high mountain basin full of huckleberries and spotted fairly fresh grizzly berry scat, but no bears. We continued on the trail around another saddle and it was then that I saw bear tracks in the dust on the trail. The tracks were headed away from us. However, due to the dry conditions, we were unable to determine their age. We began climbing slowly towards another saddle and as we approached, I looked at the peak directly to the south and spotted a promising avalanche chute. As we hiked closer to the saddle and I saw more of the avalanche chute, which was covered in huckleberry bushes, I remarked, "This looks like a great place for grizzlies." Immediately after I uttered the words, I looked at the other side of the saddle. About 30 yards in front of us was a female grizzly and her yearling cub busily eating huckleberries.

I was in the lead as we approached the saddle. I already had my bear spray out because of the awesome habitat unfolding in front of us. Upon seeing the bears we immediately froze and began whispering about a possible strategy. We obviously did not want to alert the bears to our presence. We felt we were entirely too close. Jim suggested we turn around and head back the way we came, but I did not want to lose sight of the bears. I felt if we turned around and she suddenly became aware of our presence, she could run into us with very little warning. We talked about other possibilities when all of a sudden she stood up, looked in our direction, and put her nose in the air. A photo at that time would have been incredible. However, we could not even consider taking that chance.

The bear could not see us even though we were fairly close. We were hiding behind tree branches right at the saddle and she was looking towards the sun. All of a sudden, she fell down on all fours and took off like a bolt of lightning. With her cub right behind, she crashed down the avalanche chute away from us. We pressed forward to watch. It was then that we saw a second cub following her.

I feel the strategy of not wanting to lose sight of the bears was correct. I thought we were too close to turn our backs on those bears. Obviously we were in a tight spot, and if we had made any noise, a charge was a distinct possibility. She reacted to our scent and, as often occurs in the vast majority of cases, she ran in the opposite direction.

MAY, 2004
Yellowstone National Park

Jim Cole and I were hiking in Hayden Valley. There was a sea of sagebrush, which is typical of most open areas in Yellowstone, surrounding a large island of lodgepole pine. We were moving along the edge of the trees. As we approached the end of one of the many fingers of the forested area, I looked up and saw a dark, young grizzly coming out of the trees right in front of us about 50 yards away. I got Jim's attention and we both froze. The bear glanced

B1179

at us and continued into the sagebrush (photo B1179). It showed no agitation or concern with our presence.

Since sagebrush varies in height and density, it is very easy to lose a bear in that landscape. Hayden Valley is also full of dips and knolls. Even without the sagebrush it would be easy to lose sight of the bear. We wanted to know where the bear was at all times as we made our way back to the road. We decided we would move parallel to the bear as long as it headed toward the road. In this way we would be able to keep our eyes on it for as long as possible and still be able to leave the area in a safe manner.

Because the bear was not agitated and showed no signs of aggression, we took a number of photographs (photo B1181). We saw this

B1181

B1185

B1124

B1191

bear eating parts of the sagebrush. We also saw it utilizing every aspect of this habitat, from eating grass (photo B1185) to digging up pocket gopher caches. Because of our proximity and the bear's tolerance, we were able to see things that never could be observed from a distance.

The bear slowly made its way towards the road (photo B1124). It reached a ridge overlooking the Yellowstone River (photo B1191). At this point it turned around and headed back towards the island of lodgepole. We were near the road and realized it was a perfect time to leave the bear and end our very productive hike. The strategy of keeping our eye on the bear not only made our hike safe, it provided valuable information.

AUGUST, 2004
East Side, Glacier National Park

I was hiking along a trail in the late afternoon when I ran into a group of people watching a mother grizzly and two yearling cubs eating serviceberries about 150 yards above the trail. They said that another family group consisting of a mother and two cubs-of-the-year had just crossed the trail and were now in thick cover below us. Since I was interested in observing this particular family group, I decided to hike up the trail to see if I could see them from a better angle. I also figured that the mother and two yearlings would be out for a while and if I could not find the mother with cubs-of-the-year, I could come back and watch this family.

B1137

I proceeded up the trail. I scanned the area thoroughly without any results. There was no sign of the younger family group. After 20 minutes I turned around and headed back to the group of people and the older bear family. Much to my surprise, when I rounded the corner where they had been, there were no people and no bears. The only thing I could deduce was that the older family group dropped down the hillside, crossed the trail, and disappeared into the thick cover.

I now retraced my steps up the trail to see if I could find this older family group. I scanned the same area as before and still saw nothing. I decided to sit down on a large rock next to the trail and listen for anything moving in the heavy cover below the trail. I soon heard brush moving about 80 yards below and to the left of my position. At first I thought it was either the older family group or a moose, because I had seen many moose in this same area.

Just then a bear came into view (photo B1137). Then another bear popped into view. I was totally surprised! It was the mother

B1135

and two cubs-of-the-year! They had probably been in the area the whole time I was hiking back and forth on the trail.

The female started moving towards the trail with the two youngsters close behind. She looked right at me but showed no sign of concern with my presence. Since I was still, calm, and very visible (I was now standing on the trail), I expected this reaction. Since I had a good view of her and her cubs, I did not want to change my position. Either backing up the trail or proceeding down past them would have resulted in my losing sight of them. In addition, any movement by me might have changed her behavior.

I stayed where I was and continued to take photos. As she neared the trail, she stopped periodically and ate serviceberries. Her cubs were curious but not nervous (photo B1135). She crossed the trail right in front of me (photo B1172). When she reached the other side of the trail she stopped to continue eating berries. She even turned her back to me (photo B1174). This was the most obvious sign that she did not perceive me as a threat. The bears continued moving up the mountainside until they disappeared from view.

My years of experience have taught me that keeping my eyes on the bear(s) and remaining still and calm is one of the most effective strategies for encountering bears. This incident is a prime example of the strategy's success. Quick movements and/or yelling and screaming might have alarmed the bear and produced the opposite results. Once again, seeing how a bear reacts to your presence before you act will usually determine the correct course of action.

B1172

B1174

Aware of our presence, this grizzly bear shows no sign of agitation or alarm. In many encounters this would be a good time to slowly back away, which we did.

CHAPTER 8
RETREAT

There are times when it is appropriate to hold your ground in a bear encounter. There are also times when such a strategy can make things worse. Sometimes it is very appropriate to retreat. However, the way in which you leave an area is just as important as when. Every case is different.

SEPTEMBER 1995
West Side, Glacier National Park

About 8 am Jim Cole and I started a day hike on the west side of Glacier. We were heading to one of our many favorite observation areas. This particular lookout was not accessible by a trail.

When we reached our first rest area, we saw in the distance two sibling grizzlies (probably two or three years old) and a female grizzly with a yearling cub. The siblings were wrestling and chasing each other, while the female and cub were eating huckleberries. We continued to our main lookout and saw more grizzlies. Obviously the huckleberries were plentiful and prime. We saw the female and yearling move up to a ridge and disappear. The siblings were still playing and causing quite a lot of commotion. We saw a female with two cubs-of-the-year. Then we saw another female with two cubs-of-the-year, and then another. They were all in the same vicinity, they were all eating huckleberries, and they were all visible at the same time.

The siblings began to move up to the ridge where the females and cubs were foraging. The siblings were roaring and growling as they played and chased each other. As they moved closer to the top of the ridge, the female grizzlies started to move about in a nervous fashion. They could hear the approaching juveniles but could not see them. The females were probably already stressed because of the large number of bears in such a small area.

B1020

B363

As the siblings approached, the females moved away from the commotion in different directions. One female and her cubs started up the ridge, moving closer to our location. As the siblings reached the top of the ridge they began to wrestle. They moved towards a group of trees and kept wrestling, while the female and her cubs continued moving toward us (photo B363). The cubs were in front of the female, who was taking a defensive position between her cubs and the rowdy siblings. The female and her cubs had no idea they were heading straight for us.

This was not good. The female was stressed, and if she ran into us, the outcome could be catastrophic. We had to get out of there fast, but we had to leave in a deliberate, careful manner because of all the other bears in the vicinity. We did not want to escape one family group just to plunge into another one. I took one last photo (photo B1020) and we retreated. We had our bear sprays out and ready for use as we hiked along the ridge. We saw more bears in the distance but we did not stop to determine whether they were black or grizzly. With all the bears in an agitated state due to the commotion and crowding, we did not want to hang around any longer. We reached our vehicle in a tired but elated state.

AUGUST, 1997
West Side, Glacier National Park

I took a hike to check a particular patch of huckleberries. The trail rose about 2,000 feet in elevation. It passed through thick forests and then through a number of avalanche chutes before breaking into relatively open areas. I reached my destination and saw two separate grizzlies from a fair distance. I surveyed the area for a little while longer without further success. Then I proceeded back down the trail.

B403

About a half mile down the trail, I heard a loud "huff!" I had been hiking with my eyes to the ground, watching my footing. I looked up and at about 40 feet in front of me, slightly to the left of the trail, was a grizzly that had been foraging in huckleberry bushes. I immediately froze and remained calm. The moment I froze the bear ran up the mountainside. He ran into thicker cover about 30 to 40 yards above me, and then stopped and turned around to face me (photo B403). It looked like a younger bear, maybe three or four years old. I felt the situation was safe, so I took a photo.

The grizzly began to "pop" its jaws, snapping its teeth together to produce a popping sound. This was a sign of agitation I had not experienced before. I did not want to agitate the bear further but wanted to alleviate the stress it felt. As I was facing the bear, I took one step down the trail, sideways. The instant I took that step the bear ran in the opposite direction and was lost in the thick cover. By the direction the bear went and by the noise it emitted, I surmised it went over a nearby ridge.

I obviously made a few mistakes in this encounter. I did not follow my hiking strategy. I knew I was in prime grizzly country with a readily available food source, but I was not making enough noise and I was not as alert as I should have been. Perhaps I was complacent because I had hiked through the area earlier without seeing any bears. But an hour to an hour and a half had passed from the time I had walked through the area on the way up the trail, plenty of time for a bear to enter the area or move closer to the trail. I should have been paying more attention. I slipped up.

Of course, we all make mistakes. It's part of the human condition. We can't be alert 100 percent of the time, and this fact should affect hiking strategy. That is, we should take into account that we cannot be doing all of the things we are supposed to be doing all of the time. So knowing what to do in a sudden close encounter is of the utmost importance. At least I was hiking with my bear spray out and the safety off, I remained calm when I saw the bear, and once I read the bear's reaction, I tried to reduce its agitation.

OCTOBER 1997
Going to the Sun Road, Glacier National Park

After the Going to the Sun Road closes to vehicle traffic in October, I often hike or bike up the road to observe grizzlies and diggings. During one outing I was hiking on wet pavement in a somewhat heavy snowfall. When I rounded a curve, I heard a repeated "flippity-flop" sound on the pavement. I looked up to see a grizzly running from me about 40 feet away. I was flabbergasted! I had no idea where the grizzly had come from or how close I had been to it. It made no huff or any other noise. I stopped and watched. After running about 50 yards, the bear began to walk back and forth as it continued up the road, keeping an eye on me all the way (photo B794).

The bear started digging alongside the road. As the bear moved away I also continued up the road. It finally disappeared out of sight. It was snowing but there were no tracks on the road because the snow was melting as soon as it hit the pavement. I rounded a bend and was surprised to see the bear lying down in front of a small work shed. It looked like a large dog in front of a doghouse. The bear immediately gave a low huff and got up, facing me. I stopped and remained calm. I took a few steps back, easing around the bend. The bear slowly walked away in the opposite direction. I turned around and headed back to my vehicle.

B794

This bear was radio collared, which meant it had been captured and was probably a habituated bear. The bear's behavior also indicated it was habituated, and it appeared to be a young bear.

When I initially encountered the bear, it was probably coming down the mountain onto the road. There were no diggings along the road where I first saw it. I initially followed the bear from a safe distance to observe it digging and eating. Since the distance between us increased as the bear moved further up the road, I did not technically feel that I was approaching the bear. Also, since it started and continued digging and eating in my presence, I did not feel I was affecting the bear's behavior. Seeing how quickly the bear was moving away from me, I thought by the time I came around the last bend the bear would be far ahead of me, possibly out of sight. I was wrong. I did not count on the bear lying down once it went around the bend.

The bear dictated my retreat. It was obviously going to stay on the road, and I didn't want to keep encountering it. I backed up because I had enough room to do so and I did not want to disturb the bear anymore. If the bear would have walked towards me, I would have held my ground, especially since it was a young bear. Part of my hiking strategy is to take nothing for granted, so I did have my bear spray out as I came around the bend.

SEPTEMBER, 2001
East Side, Glacier National Park

I went on a six-mile hike to check grizzly utilization of hedysarum roots. In the meadows of my destination, I saw old diggings of glacier lilies but no hedysarum diggings. I advanced cautiously because islands of dense scrub fir limited visibility.

As I approached the base of a pass, the open areas expanded dramatically. I had visibility for hundreds of yards in every direction. I looked to my left and noticed a female grizzly and cub-of-the-year busily digging roots in a rocky, flat, open area. The bears were about 80 yards away. I pulled out my camera and began taking photos. At that point, the female looked up and saw me.

I was already still and remained so. She studied me for some time (photo B1029). I did not move. She slowly moved away, while at the same time keeping an eye on me. When she disappeared behind a slight rise, I decided to leave the area because I had lost sight of her. As she moved away from the trail, she was headed in the direction that I had to go to get back to the trailhead. I felt if I waited too long to leave, she could reach the trail and I could run into her again in tighter quarters. I made noise so that she knew where I was.

Once again the encounter ended the way most do: the bears moved away. I did not investigate the digging site because I did not want to get closer to the bears. They may have been just over the rise, and I didn't want them to become agitated. This encounter happened in an open area so the bears had plenty of room to move away. Also, I remained still and calm so there was less reason for the bears to consider me a threat.

B1029

CHAPTER 9
LATE SEASON BEARS

Grizzlies encountered late in the fall may present unusual situations. As they approach hibernation, many bears appear and act sluggish. This may affect their quickness and their reaction behavior. The following three encounters are fairly typical examples of bear behavior at this time. It should be noted, however, that not all bears will exhibit these traits at this time of year.

OCTOBER, 1997
Going to the Sun Road, Glacier National Park

On a cool autumn day I parked my car at the Loop parking lot and started hiking up the Going to the Sun Road, which had been closed to vehicle traffic. As I got higher in elevation, I encountered snow on the road. I saw old bear tracks and diggings of varying ages. I was paying careful attention to the sides of the road and carrying bear spray in my right hand.

I rounded a bend and heard a loud "huff.'"About 20 feet below the road and 25 yards in front of me, a female grizzly and two yearlings were standing on their hind legs, looking at me. The second I looked, they came down and moved below me. They were not running but they moved steadily away through alders covered with snow. I watched them as they disappeared into thick cover directly below me.

This female seemed rather sluggish, perhaps because of approaching hibernation, but that doesn't mean one should be less careful. It only means that the bears may not act as fast. They can become aggressive if they perceive a person as a threat.

OCTOBER, 1997
Going to the Sun Road, Glacier National Park

This scenario was similar to the previous one except that Jim Cole was hiking with me. As Jim and I approached the spot where I had seen the female and two yearlings, we were very cautious and deliberate. After we rounded a long curve in the road, I took a peek over the steep edge and came face to face with a pair of two-year-old cubs. They were digging right at the edge of the road. I stepped back and quietly told Jim what I had just seen. We took our cameras and approached the edge. The two cubs were still there and this time we saw the mother. The bears did not seem at all startled but rather moved in a deliberate manner into heavier cover. They descended below us and disappeared.

Once again this was a family group that appeared rather lethargic. They made no huffing or any other noise. They did not appear agitated but were calm and deliberate. They may have been accustomed to people on the road and were not overly concerned with our presence.

LATE OCTOBER, 2003
East Side, Glacier National Park

One evening I received a message from Bill and Carol Smith, two bear enthusiasts from Oregon. They had been camping on the east side of Glacier and told of a good sighting of a mother grizzly and her cubs-of-the-year. The next morning I was at the trailhead by 9 am.

I had an idea of the bears' location, if they hadn't moved very far from the previous day. At the four-mile mark I started looking intensely, without success. For the next two miles I slowed my pace and stopped frequently to view thoroughly any open area. I came over a small rise at the very end of the trail and saw two cubs 70 yards in front of me. Success.

I froze, remained calm, and looked for the mother. There she was, lying to the right of the cubs, looking directly at me. She didn't move. I took out my camera and snapped a picture. She didn't take her eyes off me. One of the cubs was a little nervous and moved to the mother. The cub lay on top of her rear haunches and stared at me (photo B1081). I did not move but continued to take photos. Finally the mother and cub, realizing that I was not a threat, got up and joined the other cub to dig roots (photo B1119).

I spent the next two hours with this bear family. Eventually the cubs disappeared behind a rise and the mother moved into a shallow depression where I began to lose sight of her. I thought about moving to a better position, but without knowing where the cubs were I thought it was too dangerous. It was time to leave.

I had been very fortunate. The bears had been rather lethargic, representing normal behavior as they neared hibernation. That night it snowed more than a foot and the Going to the Sun Road closed for the season. I believe this family group was near its den and probably went in that night. I had been very fortunate, indeed.

B1119

B1081

This young habituated grizzly entertains a roadside crowd in Yellowstone National Park.

CHAPTER 10
HABITUATED BEARS

Habituation of bears is becoming a serious issue. As more people move into grizzly habitat and more people recreate in the home of the great bear, the bear ends up seeing and coming into close contact with more people. For that reason many such bears lose their "normal" wariness of people. The two main characteristics that I have recognized in habituated bears are (1): they do not run from human encounters as quickly or as often as other bears, and (2): when they are close to people they tend to pretend the people are not there. Both types of behaviors can certainly affect one's hiking and encounter strategies.

AUGUST, 1997
East Side, Glacier National Park

One morning at Many Glacier I spotted two grizzly siblings about 400 yards up a mountainside. By their sizes I guessed they were most likely two-year-olds. Since trees obstructed my view, I moved to an area that I believed was both safe and also gave me an unfettered view of their activities. I set up my tripod with a 600 mm lens and proceeded to take a few long-distance photos. The bears were eating serviceberries and rolling over rocks to check for insects and grubs.

When I am in bear country I never wear camouflage. As a matter of fact, I usually wear bright clothing. I want the bears to see me. I don't hide from bears and I don't want a bear bumping into me because it didn't see me. On this day I was wearing a white t-shirt and was in plain view of the bears. Even from a fair distance one of the bears saw me.

The bears slowly made their way down the mountainside in my direction. They both looked at me as they approached within 50 yards. They continued to eat serviceberries and periodically looked at me. Neither one showed any aggression or agitation at my presence. I

B406

remained still and calm as I took photos (photo B406). Eventually they disappeared into thick brush. Later I found out they had crossed the road, ending up at Lake Josephine. There they played on an empty tour boat at the dock.

These bears were habituated. They were used to frequenting places where people were.

During my work in Denali National Park in 1994, Jim Cole and I observed many grizzlies, mainly single young bears and females with cubs, in the road corridor. Jim deduced that these bears were hanging around the road for security from larger bears. Not once did we see a dominant male grizzly near the road. The males mostly stay in the backcountry, avoiding human contact as much as possible.

Habituated bears, or those that come near humans for any reason, may learn that humans have food, especially garbage. Not only do habituated bears appear to lose their natural instinct for avoiding humans, but if these bears become food conditioned, they may become emboldened to approach people or human areas to get food. In a high proportion of cases, these are the bears that are involved in maulings and property destruction.

SEPTEMBER, 1997
West Side, Glacier National Park

Jim Cole, his brother Billy Grant, and I reached our observation point about 7 am. We immediately saw several single grizzlies in the open areas. One of these bears was foraging for a long time. We noticed it wore a radio-collar. Later, we moved up the trail to a different vantage point and noticed that the radio-collared grizzly was moving down the hillside towards us.

We stopped hiking and remained still and calm while watching the bear. Every now and then it stopped and ate huckleberries as it slowly approached to within 35 yards of us on the trail. It then looked up and noticed us (photo B390). We remained motionless

B390

and calm. The bear's reaction was, basically, to ignore us. It moved onto the trail and, while standing on the trail, ate huckleberries (photo B393). Because the bear's reaction to us appeared neutral, we continued to stand on the trail and observe. Not once did this bear show any agitation or aggression towards us.

This appeared to be a young bear (three or four years old) and because there were many bears in the area, it may have moved towards us for security. I also believe it was the oldest surviving cub of the "Lake Five Sow." The Lake Five Sow had been tagged and radio-collared because of her associations with humans. If this were her cub, it was entirely possible that it was exhibiting behavior learned from its mother. Habituated bears tend to pass down habituated behavior to their offspring.

The bear finally gave us a last look (cover photo), slowly walked up the trail, and disappeared. The photo shows why it is a good idea to make noise when hiking. Notice the trees, thick cover, and readily available bear

B393

food sources like the red-leaved huckleberry bushes lining the trail. It is also a good example of why you should never approach a bear. The bear did not feel like we were a threat. However if we had attempted to get closer, even by one step, it may have felt trapped or threatened and events could have changed dramatically.

Even though we felt safe in this situation, I would not recommend spending time observing a bear from such a close distance. In these situations I would recommend that once a bear's reaction is observed, and the reaction is to ignore you, you should leave. You should do this by slowly backing away from the bear while at the same time keeping your eye on it. You don't want to lose sight of the bear. You want to be able to observe any change in its behavior. Once you feel that you are a safe distance from the bear (common sense dictates), you may turn around and quickly walk away. Remain alert for any other bears that may be in the area.

B1203

B851

MAY, 2001
Yellowstone National Park

Jim Cole and I had been following a mother grizzly and her two yearling cubs for a couple of days along the road between Mammoth and Norris Junction. This was the famous female bear known as "264" and her two male cubs. These bears were definitely habituated. Not only did they use the busy road corridor to possibly avoid large male bears, they also used it for ease of travel (photo B1203). They were on or within 100 yards of this road most of the time.

On numerous occasions tourists would get out of their vehicles for a better look. Sometimes groups of people would be 30 yards or less from the bear family (photo B851). The mother bear never showed any

B820

signs of aggression or agitation. She was a model of tolerance and gentleness.

One day as the family was heading north along the road corridor towards Swan Lake, they leisurely crossed the road. Vehicles going in both directions stopped, creating an open area on the road for the bears to cross. However, one woman had set up a camera on a tripod right in the middle of the road. She was in the direct path of 264 and her cubs. As the bears approached, the woman stood by her camera even though she had plenty of time to get in or behind her car.

What truly amazed me was that both the woman and the bear family retained their inertia. The woman didn't budge and the bears didn't change course. The result was photo B820. The bears came within five feet of the woman. Bear 264 didn't even glance at her. It's almost as if the bears pretended the woman wasn't even there. The tolerance and gentleness of 264 is frozen forever in this photo.

I approached the woman after the bears had crossed and continued on their way. I was fairly angry at her for letting the bears get that close—not because she could have been in danger but because she put the bears in danger. If a park official had seen how close the bears got to the woman, there was a chance, however slight, that the bears would have been removed from the ecosystem.

In any case, 264 and her family continued to educate, inspire, and thrill thousands of people for the next two years. In June 2003, 264 was struck by a vehicle. Because of the severity of her injuries, she was euthanized. She had no cubs that year. Sadly, as often happens, bears that use areas near people may face risks worse than the ones they were trying to avoid.

JULY, 2000
East Side, Glacier National Park

B748

B751

About 6 p.m. Jim Cole and I headed up the Iceberg Lake Trail to look for a grizzly that Jim had seen eating huckleberries that morning. We hiked a short distance and sighted the bear immediately. It was on the north side of the trail in some prime huckleberry patches.

As we watched, the bear moved closer to us while still concentrating on the thick, ripe "hucks." It paid little or no attention to us. At times the bear was barely visible in the thick bushes. People were walking within 20 yards of the bear and didn't know it was there. As the bear moved closer to the trail, I began taking pictures (photo B748). The light was excellent, but the sun soon dipped below the mountains and the light faded. We hiked back to camp elated at the wonderful experience.

The next morning Jim and I were up early. We wanted to find the bear and be in a good position for photographs by the time the morning sun fully hit the bruin. As we approached the area, we noticed two people rather furtively climbing above the trail. This seemed odd because they were in the exact location the bear had been the night before. As we got closer they breathlessly explained they had just run into two different grizzlies around the corner. They were bushwhacking around the bears and planning to get back on the trail further down. Jim and I rounded the corner of the trail very cautiously.

We immediately saw the bear we had photographed the night before, still above the trail but now further to the west. It was eating thick bunches of berries, exactly as it had done the night before.

I happened to look to my left. Another grizzly, much darker than the other bear, had walked onto the trail (photo B751). I couldn't believe it. The bear was only 20 yards away and wasn't paying any attention to us. It moved above the trail and also began eating "hucks." Both bears were about 25 yards from us and from each other. Both appeared to be sub-adult or small adult bears. Neither bear showed any concern over our presence. The two bears, even though rather close together, did not seem aware of each other.

All of a sudden the darker bear (we assumed it was a male) realized that the lighter bear was not only very close, but it was eating huckleberries out of its patch. With a loud huff the darker bear charged the lighter bear. The lighter bear immediately ran away in the opposite direction. Both bears ran up and around us and back down to the trail. On the other side of us, the dark bear caught up to the light bear and they collided (photo B749). In the photo you can notice the dust flying.

B749

B760

B758

You can also notice the two women in the background. They are running away, although it doesn't appear this way in the photo. When the two women rounded the corner in the trail and looked up, two grizzlies were running right at them at full speed. The women had no idea the bears lacked any interest in them. They just basically panicked. I have repeatedly said never run from a bear. However, given this circumstance, I might have run too. In any case, we never saw the two women again.

The bears started fighting. The dust was flying. There was growling. I had never seen two grizzlies fighting at such a close range, and my first thought was of a dog fight. They were really "jawing" it. Almost as soon as it started, it was over. The darker bear won. The lighter bear just sat on the trail and recuperated. A group of people came around the corner and were surprised to see a grizzly sitting in the middle of the trail (photo B760). We saw no signs of blood, which is fairly typical in bear skirmishes. Both bears were now between Jim and I and the group of people. Neither bear gave us a second thought. They were only concerned with each other.

Since the lighter bear lost, it left. The darker bear intently watched the lighter bear to make sure it left the huckleberry patch (photo B758).

More people had come around the corner and saw the darker bear in the middle of the trail. It started to move down the trail towards us and back to the original huckleberry patch. I decided I had better get off the trail. I moved below the trail to let the darker bear go by, but the embankment was steep and covered with bear grass. Bear grass can be very slippery. Since I did not want to fall down right in front of the grizzly, I got back on the trail. The bear was pretty close but I felt I didn't have any other option. Thankfully, the bear was very obliging. It got off the trail and stopped right above us (photo B753). Although we were only yards away, the bear was not concerned with our presence. It was still looking to make sure the lighter bear had gone. You can see that the bear was foaming at the mouth, just like a dog that has been in a fight. The darker bear went back to eating berries and eventually disappeared into heavy cover below the trail.

B753

Later the trail was closed. Apparently the two women who had run away had reported the incident to the rangers. At first Jim and I were upset that the trail was closed since the bears had done nothing "wrong." They had only been close to the trail. Upon further reflection, however, I thought the National Park Service had done the right thing. It wasn't necessarily the people they were trying to protect, but the bears.

It was very possible that with the number of people on the trail and their lack of bear awareness and knowledge, it was only a matter of time before someone did something stupid. Someone might have tried to feed the bears or get a picture of their kid close to a bear. In these scenarios, it is ultimately the bear that suffers. It is definitely my belief that bears are not the ones that need to be "trained" (harassed is a better term) to stay away from people or trails. Rather, it is people, including myself, who need to be *educated* about how to act in the bear's home.

We witnessed an incredible amount of unique bear behavior in these two days. The events illustrated not only how bears can interact with other bears but also how bears can interact, or not interact, with people. Both of these grizzlies exhibited "habituated" behavior. Some authorities believe that habituated bears—but not food conditioned—may actually be safer to be around. I do not necessarily prescribe to this theory. I have too much respect for these great animals to be complacent around them.

In any event, I believe Jim and I acted appropriately under the circumstances. Jim and I both had our bear spray out when the dark grizzly approached on the trail. Interestingly, I didn't notice anyone in the other group with bear spray.

Looks may be deceiving. This young grizzly looks big but we estimated his weight at about 250 pounds. Older, very large male grizzlies are rarely encountered by hikers.

CHAPTER 11
BIG BOYS

"**B**ig Boys" is the term Jim and I use for large male grizzlies. Although male grizzlies are probably the most impressive animal on the planet, they are seldom seen. Big grizzlies don't become big by hanging around people. They are incredibly intelligent, secretive, and very shy. Most people who see any grizzly usually explain their encounter with expressions such as a "huge boar," "10-foot-tall silvertip," "900-pound monster," or some other exaggeration. I have stood next to people as we watched 175-pound, two-year-old bears and heard them estimate the bears' weights at 800 pounds. From such reports you would think there are giant male grizzlies all over the place. In reality, the opposite is true. When you actually see one of these animals, you'll know it! The trick is to see one. It's basically pure luck.

Most of the time, a "big boy" becomes aware of you long before you have any inkling of its presence. If you are lucky enough to see one, chances are the encounter will be brief and not terribly exciting.

MAY, 1992
Westside, Glacier National Park

One afternoon Jim and I drove close to a large meadow where he had spooked a large grizzly the previous evening. We quietly hiked a short distance to the edge of a bank where we had a good view of a portion of the meadow below. I spotted a large, dark male grizzly about 150 yards below and to our left. He appeared to be eating grass. I took a few photos with my 300mm lens but realized I needed my 600mm lens because of the distance. I hurried back to the truck to get my lens and tripod. When I returned, Jim and I walked down closer to the edge of the meadow, set up the tripod, and began taking pictures.

B273

B272

The bear moved closer, unaware of our presence (photo B273). We could see that it was actually eating sedges. I moved my tripod to the side of the trees and took a picture. The big male heard the click of the camera shutter, lay down, and began looking around for the sound. I took another picture. He swung his head around and looked right at us. I took another picture (photo B272). Notice the impressive size of this bear's head. After hearing two shutter clicks, the bear knew exactly where we were. The third shutter click was the last straw. The bear ran directly into the thick cover of the swamp, which was the same place he had disappeared the night before. This bear was not going to stick around to determine what was going on. He displayed exactly the same characteristics of most bears his size. Once he determined there were people nearby, he ran away—fast.

MAY, 1993
South Side, Glacier National Park

Jim and I were on the trail by 8 am. We saw no bear sign, but when we came to an open marshy area about 1.5 miles up the trail, we saw a moose scrambling up the side of a mountain. We thought that was rather odd.

We continued up the trail and saw a brown-colored black bear scrambling up the same mountain, all the way to timberline. Then it occurred to us: both animals must be fleeing from a grizzly. We decided to hike higher to the open flanks of a nearby mountain for a better view. We reached a good vantage point and began to survey the area. We could see no grizzly anywhere. We decided to go down and circumnavigate the marsh to get better views of the different openings.

As we neared the marsh we entered thick cover. I was in the lead. I could now only see about 10 feet in front of me. This was nuts! I turned to Jim and said, "What are we doing?" We climbed a nearby open hillside as fast as possible. We hoped it would provide a better view of the marsh.

Jim was about two steps in front of me when we reached the open. I looked up and saw a huge furry hump about 25 yards uphill. The size of the hump made me automatically think "buffalo," but there are no bison in Glacier. Then I knew. Here was a big boy with his head down in what appeared to be a shallow swale. I whispered to Jim, "Grizzly!" The bear looked up and didn't hesitate. He fled.

It took us a few seconds to comprehend what had just occurred. By trying to be safe we stumbled right into a situation we were trying to avoid. We looked around for clues why the large male was on that hillside. We found biscuitroot all around us, along with corresponding diggings. It was a mystery why we didn't see the bear from our higher vantage point across the drainage. However, our focus had been on the marsh; the bear may have been on that hillside all along.

I had my bear spray ready with the safety off ever since we entered the heavy cover near the marsh. Knowing almost certainly that a grizzly was in the area, and knowing there were sight limitations in the terrain and cover, caused us to maintain caution and awareness. This is a strategy that works well in any hiking situation.

NOVEMBER, 2001
West Side, Glacier National Park

This story is about a non-encounter encounter, if there is such a thing. I started a 21-mile hike early in the morning. My goal was to reach a lake and then hike back before dark. There was an inch of new snow on the frozen ground, perfect for tracking, but I saw no fresh bear tracks or scat. I did find fresh mountain lion tracks.

On my way back from the lake the trail entered an open area on the edge of a large meadow. Here I noticed huge grizzly tracks in the snow, and they were right on top of my tracks. I couldn't believe it. It looked like the bear had been following me. Where was it? I studied the meadow. I backtracked the bear's tracks but soon lost them in heavy cover.

I continued towards the trailhead. Only a mile from my car I saw the tracks again. They were on top of my tracks (see photo T48 in Chapter 2). The bear may have started following me when I started hiking. I didn't know if he had been behind me by seconds or minutes or hours. All I knew was that his tracks looked the same age as mine.

It is interesting to study the photo. These are stereotypical grizzly tracks. Notice how large they are. I wear a size 11 hiking boot with a 12.5-inch sole. Also notice the long claws. The claw points on the front foot track (which has the long claws) are about four inches beyond the toe pads. This was certainly a large grizzly.

As is usually the case with a "big boy," I never saw him. I have learned that large male grizzlies like to keep track of what is going on in their territory. This includes following humans without the humans knowing it. I really don't worry about running into these large bears. I realize that if I encounter a grizzly, it is much more likely to be a young bear or a mother bear with cubs.

CHAPTER 12
BEARS ON CARCASSES

One of the most potentially dangerous situations in bear country, especially grizzly country, is a bear feeding on an animal carcass. It doesn't matter how the animal died; grizzlies don't care. Any meal containing protein and fat is an important bonanza. As a result, bears will usually protect their kills and carcasses in an aggressive manner. You should exhibit special care if you suspect a carcass in the area or if you actually see one. I have never encountered a bear on a carcass while hiking. The following cases are presented to provide an understanding of the elements of carcass utilization and associated bear behavior.

SEPTEMBER, 1995
Whitefish Range, Flathead National Forest

A friend told me there was a grizzly on a moose carcass near a Forest Service road up the North Fork of the Flathead River. Apparently a hunter had shot a bull moose and left it to rot because the antlers were not large enough. I couldn't go that day, but I called Jim and he located the bear on the carcass.

When I met Jim at the site the next morning, I could not believe what I saw. There was a grizzly lying on a mound of dirt and vegetation (photo B536). There was no sign of the moose; it was com-

B536

B359

B356

B354

pletely buried. We set up our tripods and settled in. We were not concerned about the bear's reaction to our presence. The bear was ear-tagged; later we learned it was an eight-year-old female. She was content to remain close to the carcass and did not display any agitation or aggression. We remained next to our vehicles.

The bear eventually began to uncover the carcass. A rotten odor soon permeated the air. It became obvious that one reason a bear buries a carcass is to hide the odor. Without a smell to attract other scavengers, competition is decreased. After a portion of the carcass was exposed, the bear began to eat (photo B359). Once in awhile she looked in our direction but she never moved towards us.

After consuming enough to become full, she carefully reburied the exposed portion. She methodically collected new dirt and vegetation between her two front paws, then pulled and rolled the material backwards in a clawing motion onto the carcass. With each subsequent burying she was required to gather dirt and vegetation from further and further away. The result was a larger and larger circle around the carcass that was becoming devoid of vegetation. This is a sign to watch for in bear country.

After reburying the moose, the bear yawned, scratched her face (photo B356), and lay down to sleep (photo B354). She slept on the carcass. This same sequence would happen numerous times that day. She would sleep one to two hours before starting the routine all over again. We remained at the site until the light faded that evening.

APRIL/MAY, 2002
Yellowstone National Park

The size of the carcass indicates how long a bear may stay in the vicinity. Jim and I heard that bear 264 and her cubs were on a bison carcass near a road in Yellowstone. The next morning we arrived and saw the bear family about 30 yards off the road. The bison carcass was in a small creek near the road.

As the morning progressed, more people and a few rangers arrived. The rangers made sure that people did not approach too closely. Actually there was no need to get closer. We were close enough.

Soon two bear management specialists arrived. They took ropes and other equipment from their vehicle and went down to the carcass with a ranger. They waded into the creek, tied ropes around the bison carcass, and maneuvered it towards the bank. They winched the carcass out of the creek and away from the road.

At first Jim and I were upset they were disturbing a natural situation. However, it soon became evident this was the best thing for the bears and, as it turned out, for photographers and the public in general. The park personnel dragged the carcass to the middle of a small meadow about 40 yards from the road. There the bears would be safer from traffic and we would be able to take better pictures.

The bears came out of the forest to inspect the new location of the carcass (photo B1114). It was very much to their liking, too. The area was much more accessible for feeding, and they

B1114

B906

B886

B1106

immediately began to feast (photo B906). The family group spent five straight days on the carcass.

All three bears spent various amounts of time feeding and/or sleeping on the carcass. Long naps that averaged about two hours were spent away from the carcass in the nearby trees (photo B886). From there they could view the carcass and nap in security. The mother also nursed them in these areas. Any combination of bears could be feeding on the carcass (photo B1106). Also, as documented in earlier cases, the carcass would be buried at various times. Burying was the mother's job (photo B983); the cubs never exhibited this behavior.

On the fifth day a new bear appeared. It appeared to be a dark adult male but not a very large one. As he approached, one of the cubs stood up (photo B888). The cub obviously had caught the male's scent. It turned and ran towards the mother who was also standing. They didn't hesitate. In

B983

one movement the entire family swung around and ran away.

A few seconds later the male moved in. This guy meant business. He inspected the carcass briefly, then reached down and clamped onto it with his powerful jaws. He swung his head up and started to drag what was left of the bison. We could see how much 264 and her cubs had consumed over the previous five days. They had been lucky, indeed. All that was left were skin and bones. The male dragged the remains into a group of trees where he finished it off during the night. When we came back early the next day, all the bears were gone.

If you discover a carcass while recreating in bear country, the main points to keep in mind are:

1) Bears generally bury their carcasses. Mounds of fresh dirt and vegetation should be avoided.

2) An exposed carcass will generally emit a rank odor. If you smell such an odor, a carcass is nearby.

3) Carcasses attract other animals, especially birds. A concentration of magpies, ravens, and/or eagles may indicate a nearby carcass.

4) Even if a bear is not visible on the carcass, it could still be nearby and will defend the carcass. **Do not approach a carcass.**

B888

CHAPTER 13
MAULING NEAR FIFTY MOUNTAIN

It was going to be a wonderful day, September 29, 1993. I had a good feeling about it.

Jim Cole and I had been talking about this hike for a week. Our destination was 12.5 miles away. We each carried 40-pound packs weighted with camera gear and our usual supplies for emergencies and unforeseen events. Even on day hikes we always carry equipment to spend the night in case we run into trouble.

We reached our destination at noon and saw fresh diggings all over the place. We were in the middle of a huge complex of mountain meadows. Some of the diggings were 30 feet or more in diameter. It looked as if somebody had used a Rototiller through the area.

We sat down to eat lunch near one of the diggings. It was safe. We could see 360 degrees around us for hundreds of yards. We viewed distant meadows with binoculars. We were in high spirits and felt sure, with the fresh sign, we would see a grizzly.

After eating, viewing, and taking in the incredible mountain scenery, we decided to head back. We hadn't seen any bears. Maybe it was too warm for them to be active. We were at 7,000 feet, above timberline, but all we were wearing on this beautiful fall day were shorts and t-shirts. It was about 2 pm.

Jim wanted to lead on the way back. He had just returned from Alaska and wasn't quite used to hiking at higher altitudes, since he had been working at sea level. He wanted to set his own pace. We had time. It wouldn't begin to turn dark until 7:30 or 8:00 pm. I had no objection to the slower pace. In fact, it would allow me time to periodically stop and scan the mountain slopes for grizzlies. I told Jim my intentions and we started back.

We proceeded exactly as planned. I stopped at intervals to glass the open mountainsides but didn't see anything. We climbed uphill through a series of small ledges. The ledges were interspersed with small grassy areas and stands of sub-alpine fir. After glassing, I caught up to Jim for a third time. He was about 45 to 50 feet in front of me. My eyes were on the trail, watching my footing. All of a sudden I heard a loud, long "Hissssss," like a locomotive letting off steam. Before I even lifted my head I knew what we had run into. I thought, "Here we go."

The grizzly was almost on top of Jim. I yelled for him to hit the ground. He didn't have a choice. At the same time he was heading for the dirt, the grizzly was swiping at him with its right front paw. However, since Jim was going down and moving out of the bear's reach at the same time, the bear was missing him.

I had always wondered how fast I could dispense my bear spray when the need arose. I reached for it so fast I amazed myself. I pulled the safety off and took two steps back on the trail, waiting for the bear to charge me. Everything that I had ever read indicated that when a bear is confronted with multiple threats, the bear will focus on the first threat and then go for the next. I was next. By this time Jim was face down on the ground and the bear was standing on top of him.

The first bite was to Jim's head. The bear ripped Jim's scalp wide open. Jim instinctively put his left hand above his head and the bear bit right through his wrist, breaking it, although we didn't know it at the time. The bear then bit Jim's left hip. This could have been the most disabling injury, but Jim carried his camera in a holster case on that hip and the bear ended up biting the camera instead. All of this happened very fast. Now it dawned on me that the bear did not know I was there.

I began walking towards the bear. From about 40 feet away I aimed the spray towards the back of the bear and fired a short burst. The grizzly heard the "whoosh" of the spray, looked up, and charged. I pushed down the trigger of the spray all the way and didn't let up. I aimed for the bear's face as it came at me. I could see the bear through the spray's reddish orange mist. The bear was taking a full blast of the hot pepper derivative directly in its face. Five feet in front of me the bear suddenly stopped, turned, and ran down the mountainside. It disappeared out of sight.

B278

Jim was still lying on the ground. I asked him if he was all right. He responded that he was okay. He stood up and walked up the trail about 60 yards into the shade. I followed. By the time I reached him, he had opened his pack, pulled out his first aid kit, and dumped the contents on the ground. It was then that I saw the profuse bleeding from the open gash on his head.

I found the hydrogen peroxide and poured it into the head wound. I placed all the first-aid items containing gauze on the wound. Then I opened my pack and retrieved a clean, white, long-sleeved shirt and wrapped it tightly around Jim's head. I used an ace bandage to tightly wrap the shirt. Next I treated his wrist. I took photos of Jim and the scene (photo B278) to document the incident. There was a fair amount of blood.

Our adrenaline was pumping, especially Jim's. Jim did not want to spend the night while I went for help. We discussed this option only briefly. Jim noticed his camera was missing. The hip holster was completely ripped apart. I went back to the mauling scene to look for the camera. Since my bear spray was almost gone, I took Jim's spray.

I found the camera in short order and decided to check the small group of trees where the bear had come from when Jim surprised it. In photo B278 it is the group of trees down the trail on the right. I discovered a patch of bare ground in the middle of the trees, about 10 feet off the trail that had been scratched out. My first impression was that the bear had been digging for roots when we surprised it.

I walked back to Jim and we prepared to leave. I carried Jim's camera equipment to lighten his load. Jim led the way. He was very motivated. About a half mile up the trail, near the northern top of Flattop Mountain, Jim took four Advil. He wasn't feeling much pain, but his left wrist was starting to bother him. He did not want any pain to get in the way of his mission, which was to make it out by dark.

Jim really took off. It was a challenge to keep up with him. About another two miles down the trail, we entered a large complex of meadows. I took a picture (photo B412) of Jim walking through the meadows with the Continental Divide in the background. Since I had only a small amount of bear spray left, I was hollering the entire way. We could not afford another encounter.

B412

After another two miles I caught up to Jim. He had taken off his pack and was fiddling with a rat's nest of rope. I couldn't figure out what he was doing. He threw me the rope and told me to lash his pack to mine. He got up and continued rapidly down the trail. In a few minutes I had about 80 pounds on my back and Jim was no-where to be seen. Catching up to him was going to be a challenge.

A half mile further, the trail descended downhill rather steeply. I wanted to hike faster, but I didn't want to risk a fall with a heavy pack. I kind of bumbled down the trail as fast I could. About a mile and a half later I came around a bend and found Jim lying in the trail. He had burned himself out. I thought I might have to leave him to get help even though it would be dark by the time help arrived. I started talking to him and realized he had nothing to drink since taking the Advil. He was dehydrated. I gave him a quart of energy drink and he started to eat an energy bar. Soon he got back on his feet and start hiking again. He continued to eat energy bars and he quickly regained his strength.

A mile and a half later we came to Mineral Creek. The suspension bridge across the creek had been taken down a couple of weeks earlier. I decided to just walk across the creek with my boots on. Jim, however, decided he wanted to take off his boots and socks to avoid getting them wet and to avoid any risk of hypothermia. As I began to sit down next to him, we heard a loud short hiss. I had accidentally hit the trigger on my bear spray. Jim took in a whiff of the hot pepper but thankfully the can was almost empty and there was no debilitating effect. Jim pointed out that I had now sprayed a bear and a person in the same day. We waded across the creek and continued.

About two miles farther we arrived at our vehicle. It was 7:30 pm and just beginning to get dark. I put the pedal to the metal. Luckily there were only a few cars on the road to West Glacier at the park entrance. We planned to call 911 as soon as we got there. I flashed my lights and sounded my horn as I passed cars on the way. Jim was coherent and in good spirits, considering the situation. He had lost a fair amount of blood. His shirt was totally soaked. At West Glacier I pulled up to a group of pay phones. There was one other person at the phones. I called 911 and told them what happened and that I would be driving Jim to the Kalispell Regional Medical Center. The man on the other phone overheard me. He was a doctor. He checked Jim as best he could and stated that he was doing okay. We headed to the hospital.

When we pulled up to the emergency room about 45 minutes later, there was a television news crew waiting for us. Jim told them in no uncertain terms not to film him. The emergency room personnel took over. I went outside for a brief interview with the local television station and then called my wife and told her what happened. I asked her to meet me at the hospital, and to bring a beer.

The doctors told us Jim's wrist was broken where the bear had apparently bitten right through one of the small bones. Also, Jim had a rather large hematoma at the base of his skull where some of the blood from his head wound had collected. Surgery was required. They were also bringing in a bear bite specialist to prescribe the appropriate antibiotics. Jim had slight claw scratches to his back where the griz had been holding him down with its front paw.

Park ranger Gary Moses showed up to interview us about the incident. We both emphatically stated to Gary that it was our fault for the attack and that no action should be taken against the bear, if they could even find it. Jim was taken into surgery where doctors put his wrist and arm in a cast and 22 staples in his head. It was about 2:30 in the morning when Suzi and I finally got home. What a day!

Jim's injuries completely healed over the winter. The next year we both volunteered with the National Biological Survey and did extensive observational studies in Denali National Park. The mauling had no effect on Jim's passion for grizzlies.

The two of us learned a great deal from the incident. First, bear spray works! Second, we now carry *two* cans of bear spray on our pack belts. I used most of my can during the attack. If a similar situation arises, I want a backup can ready. Third, if there are two or more people in your group, at least two people should be carrying bear spray. Jim had bear spray on his pack belt. However, he had no chance to get it out. If I hadn't also had bear spray, what would I have done? I don't want to even think about it.

In retrospect, we believe the bear was sleeping in a day bed. That would explain the scratched-out area in the trees and why Jim didn't see it. If the bear had been feeding, there was a good chance Jim would have noticed it.

Other aspects of the incident also affected our behavior and hiking strategy. Obviously we were not making enough noise. The fact that Jim got very close to the bear indicated that our noise did not alert or wake the bear. The lack of adequate noise was a result of us not hiking together, since I was in the process of catching up to Jim.

Normally when we are hiking we make enough noise through our constant conversations. We talk about whatever comes to mind, especially sports and baseball. From that day I have made a constant effort to be conscious of the appropriate times to make noise while hiking. Of course, laziness and daydreaming are common reasons hikers fail to make noise. Daydreaming is especially easy to do when hiking and I have been guilty of it many times. Only discipline can overcome these failures.

I also believe we let our guard down on the way back. Since we had encountered no bear sign on the way in, we became lackadaisical in our attention and attitude. It is always dangerous to assume that if you see nothing on the way in, you will see nothing on the way out. I do not believe we consciously took this attitude but we may have unconsciously taken it to some extent. In grizzly country, you should never take anything for granted. Arrogance and complacency can kill you.

Overall I believe the events of that day were beneficial to both Jim and me. It gave us a better understanding of a magnificent animal and of our own shortcomings. It instilled in us respect and awe that we carry to this day.

CHAPTER 14
BEARS THAT CHARGE YOU

On August 13, 1999, three people were mauled by the same female grizzly, which had a yearling cub, in two separate incidents on the Scalplock Lookout Trail in Glacier National Park. The following description of the maulings was taken from the August 19, 1999, issue of *Hungry Horse News,* a weekly newspaper that serves the park area.

A mother grizzly with a yearling cub.

A lone hiker apparently surprised the female grizzly and her cub when they were about 100 yards below him. The bear immediately charged even though the hiker tried to avoid eye contact with the bear. The newspaper reported that the hiker turned and quickly left the trail. I interpreted this to mean that he possibly ran. The bear caught the hiker as he curled into a fetal position and bit him several times before leaving. The hiker returned to the trail where he soon met two park maintenance workers with pack stock. They administered first aid, put the injured hiker on a pack animal, and started down the trail to Walton Ranger Station. One of the workers raced ahead to warn of the attack and secure medical aid.

Not long after, the remaining worker and the injured hiker were overtaken by another hiker who, along with his hiking partner, had just been mauled by the same grizzly a mile farther up the trail. This hiker had left his partner because she was unable to walk. The park worker gave the hiker his horse so the hiker could retrieve his injured partner. The park worker and first injured hiker continued down the trail. The second injured hiker went back, placed his injured companion on the horse, and made their way to the ranger station. Rescue personnel and park rangers met them on the way.

Apparently the pair of hikers encountered the grizzly family as it was moving up the trail after mauling the first hiker. Obviously the mother bear was already quite stressed from the previous attack. She charged the two hikers at full speed from about 25 feet away, mauled them, and left. All three people recovered from their wounds. No one was reported to be carrying bear spray. Elements of these incidents relate to the encounters I had a few days later.

On August 16 I took a hike in the western part of Glacier to check on a huckleberry crop. I started about 3:30 pm. After four miles I checked on the huckleberries and discovered that ripe berries were not yet plentiful. I glassed for grizzlies without success. About 6:15 pm I started hiking back to my car. Along the trail there were many avalanche chutes, and I was always very careful around the chutes because they contained thick cover and abundant food sources, including berries. With my bear spray in hand, I slowly turned the corner into one of the chutes. Earlier I had been making my coughing noise, but now I was rather quiet and alert because I was listening and looking for movement. It was about 7 pm.

All of a sudden I heard a loud "huff!" About 35 yards above the trail a female grizzly with a yearling cub ran uphill away from me and disappeared into the timber. I figured they had been eating huckleberries or, more likely, moving down the chute to cross the trail. I waited to give them time to cross the trail further down the hillside. I also thought that waiting would give them time to move away, reducing the risk of running into them again.

For about 20 minutes I picked and ate huckleberries next to the trail. Then I continued down the trail with my bear spray out, safety off, saying a loud "YO" as I hiked. I approached the next avalanche chute, slowly rounded the corner, and saw the yearling take off up-hill about 50 yards ahead of me. I couldn't see the female, but I heard her huffing. Then I heard the female tearing through the heavy brush towards me. I backed up on the trail with my bear spray pointed towards the noise in the brush. I was trying to give myself as much open area as possible to use the spray. The crashing and huffing continued in one place for a few seconds, and then the noise moved away in the direction of the yearling. Things became quiet. I couldn't believe I had run into the same bears again.

This time, instead of waiting, I proceeded down the trail, making a lot of noise and carrying my bear spray out with the safety off. I figured the bears were definitely trying to cross the trail, and I was looking for them as carefully as I could. I never saw them again.

The next morning I took a different hike to the west side of the Continental Divide in Glacier. As I approached my destination, I noticed fresh grizzly diggings of glacier lily roots. I carefully looked around and listened intently for any indication of a nearby grizzly, but I saw and heard nothing. I reached my final observation site on a 50-foot cliff overlooking a large valley with many openings (this is the same cliff from which I took photo B271 in Chapter 7).

It was 9:50 am. I took off my pack and sat down to glass the area. I took out one of my cans of bear spray from the pack holster and laid it on the ground next to me. I do this whenever I am sitting in case a bear comes into my vicinity. I viewed the entire area with my binoculars for about 20 minutes without seeing anything. I took out my food bag and had breakfast, consisting of dry food, along with a sports drink in my water bottle.

I continued viewing. About 10:40 am I heard something behind me. I quickly looked around and came face to face with a mule deer doe that was watching me from about 20 feet away. About 11 am I decided to move to higher elevations where more territory could be seen.

I stood up and started packing to leave. As I bent down to put away my food bag, I noticed a flash of brown out of the corner of my eye. I looked up and saw a female grizzly with a yearling cub coming around a small group of trees about 20 yards away. She saw me at almost the same instant, and she immediately charged.

My only thought was, "I hope that can of bear spray that was on the ground next to me is still at my feet when I look down." I had another can of spray in a pack holster, but I knew I didn't have time to grab my pack and find that spray. I looked down and there, thank God, was the other can. I reached down and grabbed it. As I pulled off the safety I said in a loud, low voice, "NOoo..." I intended to say "NO, don't come any closer," but "no" was all I got out.

The two bears immediately stopped and stood up on their hind legs. The cub was doing exactly what its mother did, standing right next to her. They were both huffing. I actually thought it was kind of cute. It was almost as if the cub was trying to be a tough guy, saying, "Oh boy, Mom, we're going to nail this guy." It was a ridiculous thought but I have learned that in life-threatening situations when things are happening very fast, the mind does not operate in the "normal" fashion.

The standing bears were about 20 feet away. I could clearly see the female's six swollen teats. She came down on all fours towards me and I immediately triggered a burst of bear spray at her face. The cloud of spray headed straight towards her but in the strong wind it made a 90-degree turn before it got to her face. Luckily, the "whoosh" sound from the can and the red cloud of spray startled both bears. They slammed on their brakes.

Both bears started moving laterally to my right. As they were moving, I glanced down the cliff. All of a sudden I realized I could climb down it. In all my previous visits to this cliff I never thought it could be climbed, but now a few, small, possible footholds looked like a stairway. I started to climb down, all the while facing the bears. There is no guarantee that bear spray will work 100 percent of the time. If it didn't work this time, I was going to bail off the cliff. However, I really didn't want to abandon my pack because there was food in it, and I was afraid the bears would get into it with dire consequences for them and possibly other hikers in the future.

The female came towards me again. About 10 feet away she stopped and stood up. I was looking up at her because I had already moved down the side of the cliff to the tops of my knees. I wasn't going to wait for her to come down. I triggered the spray and this time, because of the short distance and favorable wind direction, the spray hit her directly in the face. In a flash, she and her cub were gone.

I could hear her huffing and puffing as they ran towards the trail. Unfortunately, they were headed in the same direction I had to go to get out of there! I climbed on top of the cliff and gathered my things. Without delay I walked towards the trail. I didn't want to remain on the edge of the cliff any longer. I pulled out my other can of bear spray and took the safety off. I walked deliberately and alertly with a can of spray in each hand and yelling, "Yo bear, Hey bear." I reached the trail and hiked out without seeing the bears again.

I went to the nearest park facility to report the incident. Since the encounter occurred so close to a trail, and the bears had been heading towards it, I wanted to warn hikers there could be a rather agitated bear in the area. I found a park maintenance person and he radioed a ranger, who told me to tell him the details. I said I would as long as they wouldn't publicize the incident. He agreed, and I described what happened. The park service did not close the trail because they believed the bears had left the area right away.

There are some facts common to the encounters of August 13, 16, and 17. Each encounter involved a female grizzly with a single yearling cub, but since the distances between the encounters were so great, it was highly unlikely the bears were the same. Each encounter took place on or near hiking trails in good daylight on warm days. Beyond these similarities, each encounter differs and should be analyzed separately.

The one aspect that really stands out about the incidents on August 13 is that no one had or used bear spray. The newspaper described the victims as "experienced hikers who have traveled extensively in the backcountry of Glacier National Park. All were aware of the procedures to follow while hiking in bear country." Something about their encounters didn't make sense to me. For example, if they were experienced, why did one of them possibly run? What were the "procedures" they were aware of? Most importantly, why didn't they have bear spray? There are a lot of other questions. However, I wasn't there and I can't second-guess what they did in the intense seconds of the encounters. Nonetheless, we can all learn from the events of that day and my encounters during the following days.

Many bear attacks that seem to lack a logical reason are blamed on the "unpredictable" nature of the grizzly bear when, in fact, there is a logical explanation. The pair of hikers who ran into the female grizzly and yearling on the 13th had no way of knowing what had transpired just a moment earlier. They encountered a grizzly that was already very agitated and stressed, and not because of anything these hikers did. How many bear attacks have occurred, for example, because a grizzly has just had an altercation with another bear? Due to our lack of knowledge about what happened earlier, we blame it on the bear by saying the grizzly is unpredictable. In my case, the second time I ran into the bears on the 16th, I knew the reason why the female was so agitated and stressed.

My encounters of the 16th and 17th were different in other ways, too. First, I am an experienced hiker who has traveled extensively in the backcountry of Glacier National Park. Second, I was carrying bear spray. As a matter of fact, I already had it out before each encounter. However, what I think is most important is that I had a personal response and hiking strategy. When I neared the first avalanche chute on August 16, I assumed that a bear could be nearby.

Also, I had encountered many bears previously so I had the luxury, if you want to call it that, of experience. It is easy for people to tell you how to react, but you can never be certain of how you are going to react when you encounter a bear. Preparing yourself by going through the possibilities over and over again in your mind will help. I hope reading this book will help. Keep in mind that ones' chances of being killed in an auto accident on the way to the park are greater than being killed by a bear in the park. Bear maulings are exceedingly rare. However, we should not let this fact lull us into a false sense of security. Assuming that a bear encounter can never happen to you is not a good strategy.

I believe the female grizzly and yearling that I encountered on August 16 were trying to cross the trail to get to lower elevations where the huckleberries were more plentiful. I believe I should have waited longer after the initial encounter before continuing on the trail. By waiting longer I may have avoided running into them a second time. I'll never know. It was purely a judgment call based on experience and common sense.

When I encountered the bears the first time, I froze and remained calm. They left the area. The second time I ran into the bears, the female's reaction was obviously different. I initially froze but circumstances dictated that I move back. I did so in a calm and deliberate manner, not a sudden or panicked manner. If I had started yelling or running or did something that the bear could have interpreted as threatening or aggressive, the outcome might have been different.

Over and over again, I have discovered that the most important common thread to safely ending an encounter is the ability to remain calm. This is easier said than done. However, it appears to be of the utmost importance, not only to reduce the bear's perception of a possible threat, but because it helps you think more clearly in an otherwise stressful situation.

My encounter on August 17 was different in many ways. First, the female grizzly and yearling cub ran into me instead of the other way around. Second, I had no room to maneuver. Third, I did not have my pack on. This was of concern for two reasons: (1): if I left the pack, the bear could have found my food, and (2): I lacked the protection that backpacks offer if a bear makes contact. For these reasons you should never take off or throw your pack towards a bear to distract it.

This grizzly was very surprised to see me. I'm convinced she didn't know I was there. Even though I had never before seen a grizzly so close to the observation point, I was somewhat prepared for such an occurrence. I had a can of bear spray next to me simply because always doing so is part of my hiking strategy.

My personal response strategy always includes thinking about options. The more options available, the more likely you will remain calm. Using bear spray is always an option, but it is not one that I like to use. However on the 17th I was glad to use it. The cliff-climbing option also proved its usefulness in two ways. It was a way out if the bear spray didn't work, and most important, even though I didn't climb down the cliff, being aware of that option helped me remain calm and concentrate on the events in front of me.

Some authorities recommend avoiding direct eye contact with a bear. This advice has been a bone of contention with me for a long time. If you run into a grizzly, the first thing you're going to do is look in its eyes. It's instinctive. I do it, and I think all animals do it. Besides, I strongly believe the other important thing to do when you encounter a bear, besides freezing and remaining calm, is to keep the bear in sight. In my encounters on both the 16th and 17th, I kept the bears in sight as long as I possibly could. I lost sight of the bears only because of their movements, not mine. I never turned my head or looked away in order to avoid making direct eye contact.

I do not believe that direct eye contact is a negative action. It is much more important to keep the bear in good view and watch its behavior. Turning your head to avoid eye contact may cause you to lose track of the bear or miss an important behavior. It may also make you appear to be intimidated, which, depending on the bear (a young bear, for example), may make the situation worse. I agree that trying to "stare down" a bear is not a good idea, but worrying about simple eye contact may interfere with other, more important strategies or tactics.

After my encounter on August 17 I asked the rangers not to publicize my incident. I thought another reported incident would give

*A two-year-old grizzly cub stands to get a better
view of hikers in Glacier National Park.*

the public the idea that the grizzlies of Glacier were acting in abnormal ways. I remembered that August 13 was the 32nd anniversary of the infamous "Night of the Grizzlies" when two girls in Glacier were killed by separate grizzlies on the same night. Any media comparison to that night would be tempting but totally without merit. I now think that asking for no publicity was a mistake. Educating the public about how I avoided possible injury by using bear spray would have served a valuable purpose.

As I continue my observations and studies, I am always learning something new. Sometimes I gain new information that does not follow conventional wisdom. For example, the more I think about my encounter of August 17, the more I believe the mother bear's act of standing up may have been an attempt to "intimidate" me off the cliff. This belief flies in the face of accepted "facts" that a bear standing up is only trying to get a better sense of the situation and that standing is a "neutral" posture. If the mother grizzly had completed her charge and made contact with me, I think both of us would have gone over the cliff. I believe the bear sensed that outcome and adjusted her tactics. That is why she stopped a few feet from me on the final rush and stood up. She was hoping I would go over the cliff. It would eliminate the perceived threat while keeping her and her cub safe. I cannot prove this theory but it makes sense.

*A two-year-old grizzly cub is focused on hikers
while its mother eats serviceberries. Even though the
mother bear seems to be ignoring the hikers, caution
must be maintained at all times.*

The author's wife Suzi demonstrates bear spray. The spray disperses rapidly into the air and may not be visible even though it remains extremely potent.

CHAPTER 15
BEAR SPRAY

As explained in Chapters 13 and 14, bear spray has saved my hide in two extreme situations. Those were the only times I have used bear spray on bears. I have carried bear spray ever since I began observing grizzlies in 1985. I heard about the spray through various reports but it was not yet available to the public. I called the developer of the product, Bill Pounds, founder of Counter Assault. We had an informative conversation and he sent me a can. I still have that can on my shelf.

The purpose of bear spray is to deter or stop an aggressive or charging bear. It is a mixture of specific ingredients contained in a canister under pressure. The contents are released through a trigger mechanism. The active ingredient is a derivative of capsicum peppers, which are among the hottest peppers known to man. Capsaicin and the major capsaicinoids are the major components. The ingredients cause a hot sensation, inflammation, and an almost immediate irritation to the skin, eyes, and respiratory system, especially the nose.

A sprayed bear suddenly has difficulty smelling, breathing, and seeing, and the bear responds with a "flight" reaction. I believe a sprayed bear forgets its objective to eliminate a perceived threat or attain a predatory goal and reacts instead to the sudden impairment of its life-sustaining functions. The bear flees in order to obtain relief from what it perceives as a more serious threat. This analysis cannot be proven in any real way. It is based purely on my own experience and observations.

The key points to successfully using bear spray
1) **Know how to use it:** Test the spray ahead of time with a real can or with a training canister. Make sure you practice how to quickly and efficiently remove the safety tab. Understand the spray's duration, distance, and dispersal pattern.

2) **Be willing and able to use it:** in an extreme encounter, hesitation can be disastrous. Remember, all encounters are different. Be prepared for any situation, including more than one bear.

3) **Have it readily accessible:** Always carry it in an outside holster where you can grab it in a second, and in any potentially dangerous situation, carry it in your hand with the safety off. Don't carry it inside your pack. In a bear encounter you don't have time to get anything out of your pack.

4) **Spray a warning blast when an aggressive bear is 40 or 50 feet away.** Ideally, an approaching bear enters the cloud of spray 25 or 30 feet away. This distance will give the bear adequate time to inhale the spray before it reaches you.

5. **If the bear continues through the warning blast, keep spraying, directing the spray at the bear's face or a little below it, as the spray tends to billow upwards.** *The spray must make contact with the bear's nose, eyes, and mouth.* You may have to adjust the spray direction to compensate for wind blowing the spray.

6) **Spray until the bear runs away or until you can safely retreat.** Every situation is different. Short bursts of spray may work, as in Chapter 14, or sustained spraying may be needed, as in Chapter 13. Distance from the bear, the bear's reaction, and environmental factors such as wind and brush will determine spraying tactics.

Bear spray

Hip holster for bear spray

If a charging bear has been sprayed only at very close range, it may still make contact because the spray takes a moment to affect the bear's senses. If contact is made, you should drop to the ground, lie flat, and clasp your hands over the back of your neck. The bear will probably leave once the spray takes effect.

Don't use the spray for anything other than a threatening bear. This point may seem obvious, but people have used bear spray like mosquito repellent. They have sprayed their kids, packs, tents, and inflatable boats. When used in this manner, bear spray can potentially become a bear attractant because of its smell.

Counter Assault, the bear spray that I carry, is the only bear spray I know that has actually been tested in controlled situations. It has been tested at the University of Montana on grizzly and black bears. When the trigger is engaged, it projects the pressurized active ingredients in an expanding cloud or cone-shaped pattern. The spray is an orange or reddish mist that extends 30 to 40 feet in windless conditions. The chemicals remain suspended in the air for a brief time. This means that the bear can run into the spray even though the bear was not within range when the canister was first fired. It also means that if the wind is blowing in your face, you may be exposed to the spray.

Criteria for an effective bear spray

1) **Time of the continuous spray:** Holding down the trigger until the canister is empty should take *at least six seconds*. With anything less, I probably would not have experienced a successful outcome in the Fifty Mountain story (Chapter 13). Canisters capable of longer spray durations might have some spray remaining after an encounter; reserve spray would be good to have for the hike out.
2) **Range in windless conditions:** The spray should extend 25 feet or more, and the farther the better.
3) **An expanding cloud or cone-shaped spray pattern.**
4) **Capsaicin and related capsaicinoids** (*not* oleoresin capsicum) as the active ingredients: The active ingredient should be one to two percent of the total ingredients.

5) **Minimum net weight of 225 grams or 7.9 ounces.**

6) **Registered by the Environmental Protection Agency (EPA) or by Canada Health:** Registration will be indicated on the label. Registration insures the spray is bear spray. Registered bear spray can be taken between Canada and the United States. (Note: personal defense, law enforcement, and military sprays are not bear sprays. Their active ingredients are not powerful enough for bears, and they often spray in a tight stream.) Do not use "pepper spray." Use only EPA-approved "bear spray." The word "bear" will be in the labeling, such as "bear spray," "bear deterrent spray," and "for defense against charging bears."

7) **Recently manufactured.** Some bear sprays have an expiration date on the canister because the internal pressure decreases over time, just like the pressure in a fire extinguisher. As pressure decreases, the spray's range diminishes. The active ingredient in the spray also loses some of its potency over time. To be safe, don't use bear spray more than four years old.

There are a few reports of sprayed bears coming back to attack again. It is difficult to assess these reports. Perhaps the bear was not adequately sprayed, or perhaps the spray was inadequate. Before the EPA regulated bear sprays, there were at least 15 brands on the market; today there are only four.

Whatever bear spray you choose, it is imperative to understand that bear spray is not "brains in a can." You cannot skip down a trail without any worries because you are carrying bear spray. Such foolishness is similar to hikers I have seen wearing "bear bells." They actually believe a bear will hear these tiny little bells and move away. Many locals jokingly refer to bear bells as "dinner bells." The bells are basically worthless. They give most people a false sense of security, and consequently people are not paying attention to terrain, cover, sign, or anything else which would indicate the need to take special precautions. Bear spray is also worthless unless it is accompanied by a basic knowledge of bear ecology.

Bear spray plays an important role in any hiking strategy. I never hike in bear country without it. I always carry two cans. I have never been in a situation where I needed to use both cans. However, as related in Chapter 13, I did empty a can in an encounter and had no backup for the hike out. I carry both cans in holsters on my pack belt where they are easily accessible.

The major factor in dispensing spray is handling speed. The spray should be carried in a place that is easily reached in a stressful situation. I believe hip holsters are the best way to carry bear spray because most of the time when hiking your hands are close to your hips. However, I have seen people wearing chest holsters. In my opinion such holsters would require raising your hands to your chest and possibly getting your hands entangled in your pack's shoulder and chest straps. But whatever holster a person feels most confident with should be used.

Whenever I sit down for more than a couple of minutes I always take one can out of its holster and place it next to me. No matter what I am doing, I make sure my bear spray is accessible.

Many times I carry the spray in my hand with the safety off, especially when I am hiking by myself (not recommended). When traveling through thick cover, near streams, waterfalls, or in other suspect situations, it is important to have the bear spray out and ready to use. It should also be ready if you believe your noise may not be effective in alerting bears of your presence. When camping in the backcountry, I keep a can next to me while sleeping. I also keep a can inside my sleeping bag. Many of these strategies may seem overly cautious. However, if you are going to carry bear spray, handling it should become second nature.

Whatever hiking strategy you develop, and I hope bear spray is part of that strategy, it is incumbent that you develop a routine and stick with it. When an encounter goes badly, events happen fast. Usually the less thinking required the more effective your reaction will be. For example, let's say you carry the bear spray in your hand with the safety off. Then every time you carry the can in your hand, the safety should be off. Don't carry it in your hand sometimes with the safety off and other times with the safety on. It'll just be poor luck to have a sudden encounter at close range, depress the trigger, and nothing happens because the safety was on. But if you usually hike with the bear spray in your hand with the safety on, continue hiking with the safety on. Jim hikes this way.

Another word of caution: carrying bear spray with the safety off requires a little care. You don't want to inadvertently spray someone or yourself. I have sprayed Jim twice and myself twice. Being sprayed is very unpleasant. Discomfort and a burning sensation can last up to 45 minutes. If spray is on your hands and you rub your eyes, your eyes will burn like crazy. The spray can cause burn marks on exposed flesh. Flush sprayed areas with plenty of water. However, the spray has no long-term effects on people or bears

So there are risks to using bear spray. The alternatives, however, pose greater risks. I have talked to many people who say, "A 44 bullet between the eyes will solve any problem with a bear." Not surprisingly, none of these people have had extreme, close encounters. After I actually had a close encounter, I realized nothing could have prepared me for the real thing. Events happen very fast. If someone believes they can draw a gun and make an accurate killing shot on a charging bear in a few seconds or less, they are not being realistic. It can be done but it takes luck. If they only wound the bear they may be mauled anyway, and they've created a wounded bear which is very dangerous. If they are successful, they have a dead bear on their hands. Bear spray takes far less accuracy to be successful and it is not lethal. Guns are not legal to carry in national parks; bear spray is legal.

The only other alternative is to carry nothing. Most people choose this option not from a conscious decision but from lack of knowledge. A few people do make this choice because they believe bear spray is unnatural or they believe they can talk their way out of a bad encounter. Some people believe they can always play dead and avoid injury.

People believe what they want to believe. I have too much respect for bears to believe I can talk my way out of every situation. I also really do not want to play dead in front of a bear. If you play dead too early, you could invite a bear to come up to you out of curiosity when it might have stopped or gone away. If it is a predatory bear (very rare but possible), you might have just invited it to dinner. You only play dead when a non-predatory bear is about to make contact with you or has made contact with you. But how do you tell the difference between a predatory and non-predatory bear? Suffice it to say, I don't want to play dead with any bear, although if all else fails in an encounter strategy, it is a last option worth trying.

Bear spray should be an integral part of anyone's hiking strategy. It is an integral part of mine. Of course, it is better to use hiking strategies that avoid spraying situations. The real value of carrying bear spray is that it gives you another option and, if necessary, another course of action. Having bear spray ready to use helps you stay calmer, and as stated many times, staying calm in a bear encounter is your best response.

A grizzly is always exciting to see. A mother nursing her cubs is a real treat.

CONCLUSION

The information in this book has been presented for three major reasons. First, I hope that through the encounters I have described one can see the grizzly is not the horrible beast that humans have portrayed for centuries. Rather, the great bear is an intelligent and tolerant animal. It should be respected.

Every bear encounter is different. Weather, terrain, time of year, time of day, food resources, and other variables all play a role in how a bear will react to your presence. More importantly, how you react to the bear's presence can be decisive. For this reason it is incumbent upon anyone venturing into grizzly habitat to understand not only the many factors that affect bear behavior, but to understand your own self. This understanding can only come from field experience. You can read as much as possible, which is always helpful, but until you actually experience what you read about, you cannot gain the insight necessary to make proper decisions.

This does not mean I encourage people to go out and try to have close encounters. If the proper encounter strategies are not utilized, an encounter can turn dangerous very fast. An encountered bear will usually turn and run, but if it feels threatened in any way, a grizzly can react defensively in a sudden and violent manner. I want people to observe grizzlies in a safe manner. Observe how they react to other bears. Observe how they react to other animals. Observe how and what they eat.

The second reason for this book is to give people an understanding of bear habitat and the awareness needed to avoid close encounters. Being alert at all times to food resources, sign, noise, and anything else that might indicate the great bear's presence must be a common component of any hiking strategy. Remember, complacency and arrogance can kill you. The more times you hike without any incident, the more likely an incident will happen. You can never let down your guard.

Even though you may take all the precautions, close encounters can still occur. This brings us to the last reason for this book: what to do when a grizzly is encountered in a situation that could end in an unfavorable result. I hope, through my many experiences described in this book, you understand that every encounter is different. There is no guarantee that your encounter will be like any I have described. Expect the unexpected. That's why it is so important to develop an effective encounter or personal response strategy based on events unfolding before your eyes.

The key component is keeping a level head. Don't panic. That's why "freeze and remain calm" works in most situations. On the other hand, if you are rounding a bend in a trail and see a grizzly running at you at a full charge, "freeze and remain calm" might not be the proper response. Carrying and being able to use bear spray eliminates a lot of undesirable options and unnecessary thinking.

An important source of information is available at the national parks. Information on hiking safety and bear behavior can be obtained at the entrance stations, visitor centers, and ranger stations. One of the most important resources, I believe, is the bear ranger programs in Yellowstone and Glacier national parks. Bear rangers can usually be found at roadside "bear jams" in Yellowstone and along the trails in Glacier. These rangers help provide opportunities to observe bears in a safe environment, and they share knowledge and answer questions about these magnificent animals.

The primary goal for most people entering grizzly country is to enjoy and discover the wonders of the wilderness. Even if no bears are sighted, most people will bring back vivid memories of spectacular scenery and pristine places. These memories and experiences are what they are because humans are not in control in these places. Experiences in such places become exhilarating. They tend to draw you back. I always want to go back. Maybe I'll run into you one day on the trail. Maybe we'll both be fortunate to share a sighting of the great bear.

After we exchanged acknowledgments,
this grizzly continued to peacefully eat.

Photo of the author in Glacier National Park by Chuck Bartlebaugh.

ABOUT THE AUTHOR

After receiving his B.A. degree in mathematics at the University of Minnesota and a J.D. degree from William Mitchell College of Law, Tim Rubbert went to work in the insurance industry where he became disillusioned with the corporate lifestyle. In 1989 he completed the PROBE secondary education program at the University of Colorado. Since 1985 he has devoted his life to the study, observation, and photography of grizzly bears. Tim has hiked various areas from Grand Teton National Park to Denali. He has hiked every trail in Glacier National Park and most of the trails in the Whitefish Range and the northern portion of the Great Bear Wilderness in Montana. He has also hiked extensively in the Greater Yellowstone Ecosystem. In the last 20 years, Tim has hiked more than 30,000 miles and experienced more than 2,000 grizzly sightings in the lower 48 states.

During his extensive travels, Tim has made a point of:

- Concentrating on backcountry observation to learn as much about grizzlies as possible with a minimum of intrusion.
- Focusing mainly in the Northern Continental Divide Ecosystem.
- Documenting numerous backcountry encounters with grizzlies.
- Learning and teaching others about the proper use of bear spray, which he has had to use twice.
- Performing volunteer work with the National Biological Survey, observing grizzly bears in Denali National Park, Alaska, in 1994
- Working with the Center for Wildlife Information, educating people on bear avoidance.

Tim has conducted grizzly bear slide presentations in Alaska, British Columbia, Idaho, Wyoming, Minnesota, and Montana. He has guided educational hikes on Big Mountain near Whitefish, Montana, and has archived an extensive collection of grizzly bear and other wildlife and scenic photos. He has also instructed classes at Flathead Valley Community College in Kalispell, Montana, on grizzly habitat and behavior. Tim lives in grizzly country in Montana.

Bears and Bears and Bears!

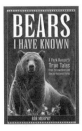

Bears I Have Known
By Bob Murphy

A former park ranger relates his most memorable experiences with bears. These first-hand stories are great entertainment and an inside look at bear management in our national parks.

Great Wyoming Bear Stories
By Tom Reed

The first-ever collection of the best bear tales from all across Wyoming, including Yellowstone and Grand Teton national parks. "An immensely valuable book for understanding and living with Wyoming's bears.
—*Laramie Daily Boomerang*

Great Montana Bear Stories
By Ben Long

Maulings, close calls, and even humorous escapades are all found in these stories, complete with discussions about how to hike, camp, and live safely in bear country. "A must-read for all lovers of wilderness."
—*Missoulian*

The Only Good Bear
By Jeanette Prodgers

A fascinating collection of bear stories that were reported in early newspapers on the western frontier. Valuable historic accounts of grizzly and black bears. "Jam-packed with information. If you enjoy good bear stories, this is the book for you."
—Larry Kaniut, author of *Alaska Bear Tales*